SQL and Relational Databases

The **DATA BASED ADVISOR**® Series
Lance A. Leventhal, Ph.D., Series Director

SQL and Relational Databases

Søren Vang

Microtrend™ Books
San Marcos, California

Originally published in Danish as *Relationsdatabaser og SQL*, Copyright©
1989 by Teknisk Forlag A/S (Danish Technical Press) Copenhagen, Denmark.

Library of Congress Catalog Card Number: 90-53256

ISBN 0-915391-42-2

Microtrend™ Books
Slawson Communications, Inc.
165 Vallecitos de Oro
San Marcos, CA 92069-1436

Printed in the United States

Edited by Lance A. Leventhal, Ph.D., San Diego, CA

Interior Design by Sandy Mewshaw
Cover Design by John Odam, Design Associates

1   2   3   4   5   6   7   8   9   10

Contents

Contents

Tables

Programs

Figures

Preface

Databases help make many aspects of our modern lifestyle possible. However, we rarely notice them; all we see are the results of their use. When you go to the supermarket, a checker passes your purchases over an optical reader that records and prints the item names and prices. Finally, it prints the staggering total! After you recover from the shock, you run your credit card through an electronic reader. You can thus pay for the groceries and perhaps also get some cash and a few headache relieving tablets. The optical reader is a clever invention, but it is of no use without a database to back it up. Similarly, your credit card is useless without database support (and enough money to eventually pay the bill).

Banks, government agencies, airlines, department stores, utilities, car rental agencies, insurance companies, hospitals, schools, and many other organizations use databases extensively to handle large amounts of data. Such data processing is essential to providing the services we expect on a daily basis.

This book deals with the procedures required to obtain information from a database. It describes a standard way to ask for precisely the data you want and to manipulate it properly.

There are many types of databases. We focus on a particular one, the *relational database*. We chose it because of its widespread use and sound theoretical basis. The relational database's unique combination of power and flexibility has led to many applications in business, education, finance, government, industry, nonprofit institutions, the professions, science, and engineering.

A key factor in the relational database's success is the availability of a standard specification and a standard user interface. The user interface provides a way to request information on any of a variety of computers or on networks involving many types of computers and software. Standardization means that one formulation will do the job on a mainframe, minicomputer, workstation, or personal computer.

The standard here is SQL (Structured Query Language), originally developed by IBM. Both the American National Standards Institute (ANSI) and the International Standards Organization (ISO) now have published specifications for it.

This book deals with SQL and relational databases generically rather than focusing on a particular product. The database market is volatile, and many products are currently in use. We discuss specific examples from such popular systems as Oracle, SQL/DS, and the OS/2 Database Manager.

The book assumes that readers are familiar with both computers and databases. It is thus suitable for intermediate-level courses in data processing, information or decision sciences, computer science, computer information systems, or management information systems. It should also be of interest to analysts, programmers, consultants, VARs, OEMs, vendors, system integrators, teachers, and advanced users. SQL and relational databases will become even more important in the future as distributed and networked systems become commonplace.

Finally, I would like to thank Tove From Jørgensen of the Danish Technical Press in Copenhagen, Steen Rasmussen of IBM in Denmark, and Jørgen Holm Nielsen of the Technical College in Copenhagen for many useful comments. Frank Bason did the English translation, Lance Leventhal the English editing and some updating, and Sandra Mewshaw the final production. Professor John Atkins of West Virginia University provided a technical review of the English version.

Søren Vang

Overview

Chapter 1 briefly describes the history of the relational database and SQL. It also defines basic terms and presents the major example used throughout the book.

Chapter 2 introduces tables, the fundamental data structure of relational databases. It shows how to create tables and describes the data types and other features SQL provides for working with them. It also discusses how to revise table structures.

Chapter 3 describes the primary tasks involved in manipulating real or **base** tables, i.e., data entry (insertion), changing (updating), and deletion. The chapter also discusses **views** or **virtual tables,** defined subsets of base tables. They help focus the user's efforts, provide security, and allow for structural changes.

Chapter 4 covers ways in which the DBMS controls the database. Not everyone needs or should have the same access to data. The chapter describes the options SQL provides for designers and administrators in terms of privilege levels and the granting and transfer of rights.

Chapter 5 covers techniques used to store and retrieve data. It describes indexing and presents its advantages and disadvantages. It focuses on B^{+}-tree indexes. The chapter also explains how to keep related data close together physically through clustering.

Chapter 6 deals with determining and analyzing the database's status. It focuses on the system catalog, the primary tool for status management.

Chapter 7 describes normalization. The division of databases into tables can have a major effect on storage requirements, ease of maintenance, and the ability to share data among varied applications. Normal forms provide a well-defined way to split tables into independent units. There are tradeoffs here, as more tables often make operations take longer and some redundancy can make tables easier to use.

Chapter 8 deals with database integrity, that is, avoiding improper or inconsistent changes. They can occur because of user actions or because of SQL's limited ability to support connections within and between tables. The chapter also discusses concurrency issues and ways to recover damaged data.

Chapter 9 deals with embedded SQL, statements that are incorporated into an ordinary high level programming language. The combination allows developers to write programs for users who have neither SQL experience nor any knowledge of the database's structure. The chapter contains a large example of an embedded program based on the C language.

Chapter 10 describes special SQL-based tools and systems, including OS/2's Database Manager. The focus is on its Query Manager. The chapter also discusses screen design tools, using Oracle's SQL*Forms as an example. Such systems provide the ability to build applications for a wide variety of users.

Chapter 11 deals with database architecture, the relationship between the database viewed as tables (the logical structure) and the physical storage. It describes how the two fit together. It also presents more details on how searches are actually performed and how indexes and clusters are implemented.

Chapter 12 covers computer configurations. It begins with single-user and multiuser systems that store and handle data in one location. It then discusses distributed systems that divide the data among several locations, thus decreasing communications requirements and increasing local self-sufficiency while still providing organization-wide access to information.

The appendixes describe the data (table contents) used in the major example and the conventions used in the book.

The book also contains a glossary, a bibliography, and an index.

1

Relational Databases

1.1 Historical Background

Commercial database managers first appeared in the late 1960's. Among them was IBM's landmark hierarchical database management system IMS (Information Management System).

Early in the history of data processing, a few isolated standard functions and routines appeared. During the 1960's, developments accelerated. More applications appeared, involving ever larger amounts of information. Organizations needed to centralize their data and gain faster and more varied access to it.

Such centralization had the following goals:

- Reducing the number of people required to maintain data.

- Allowing departments to share data.

- Allowing many people to share programs.

- Introducing standards for data organization and information retrieval.

- Avoiding inconsistencies and errors, such as double ordering of inventory or double sale of stock.

The new problems raised by centralization included:

- Greater complexity and interdependence of data.

- Larger and more complex programs needed to process data and serve users.

- New needs for security and privacy in multiuser applications.

- Greater dependence on computers and software, hence more serious consequences of operating problems and system errors. The advantage here is that one can always blame the computers for everything that goes wrong!

The physical solution was a large mainframe. Remote terminals were available for individual users, but lacked local processing power. The main CPU (central processing unit) did all the computing.

On the administrative side, the centralization of data processing meant that organizations needed separate departments for this function. Such departments had three groups of employees:

Database Administrators (henceforth abbreviated as DBAs), who are responsible for overall policy such as creating databases, managing security, and determining development strategy.

Applications Programmers, who set up, maintain, and develop the programs required to meet the organization's data processing needs.

Systems Operators, who ensure the proper functioning of both the hardware and the software on which the database programs run.

Outside the data processing (or information systems) department, **end users** employ the applications controlled by the administrators and programmers.

The appearance of minicomputers and personal computers (PCs) in the 1970's and 1980's created a countertrend away from centralization. The new principle became "One person, one machine".

The 1981 introduction of the IBM PC made low-cost small machines a standard fixture in offices, schools, hospitals, factories, and other locations. The PC quickly became a powerful, serious tool, thanks in part to such popular applications as spreadsheets, word processors, graphics and drawing programs, programming languages, and database management systems.

The problem also arose of how to allow PCs to communicate with each other and work with central mainframe resources. Local area networks (LANs) soon became a widely used method.

The basic problem is one of making different types of software and hardware communicate. One solution is the OSI (Open System Interconnection) model standardized by both IEEE and ISO. IBM has developed its own set of rules (the Systems Application Architecture or SAA concept). It allows applications to run on equipment ranging from mainframes through minicomputers, workstations, and personal computers. Developers need not worry about what equipment users have in a particular situation or environment.

The SAA concept allows developers to write application programs on a PC and execute them on a mainframe or visa versa. It also allows for the transmission of displays from one type of computer to another and the storage of data on different machines (or even types of machines). In other words, the SAA concept means total integration of software and hardware throughout an organization, thus simplifying development, coordination and combination of results, planning, and training.

1.2 Other Types of Databases

IMS (Information Management System) is a **hierarchical database** management system. It has two key features. One is the close relationship between the language used to write the database software and the physical organization of the data. The other is the hierarchical relationships among individual data sets (tables).

The hierarchical data structure involves a formalized superior or inferior relationship between individual data sets, reflecting the organization of a company (Figure 1-1). The relationship depends on the connections between data sets via their addresses (pointers). The result is like a military chain of command with fixed patterns of communication and formal rank ordering of units.

The problem with a hierarchical structure is a rigidity that hinders working flexibly with stored data. The structure of the database and the pointers that are implemented determine the kinds of operations you can readily perform. If the database has not been prepared in advance to recognize a relationship, the connection cannot be utilized without first establishing the necessary pointers.

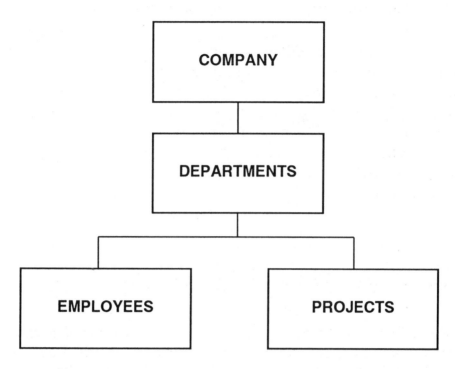

Figure 1-1. Hierarchical organization of a company.

In the hierarchical structure, the chain of command is fixed. For example, to find all projects in a department, one must follow the pointers defined for the relationship.

The rigidity (and thus also limited searching options) that characterizes the hierarchical database is relaxed somewhat in the network database. Instead of following a single chain of command (from the top down), we can now also search across the structures. However, we can still use only established paths.

A common characteristic of both types of databases is that the user cannot just add or delete data. He or she must also change the pointers that link the data. Working with hierarchical and network databases, therefore, means working not just with data but also with structural and physical elements.

Another characteristic is that such databases are neither flexible nor user-friendly. The user must write programs to perform searches that have not been predefined.

Note, however, that the rigid structure leads to fast execution because no decisions are necessary. High speed is one reason why IMS remains in wide use today.

Furthermore, the **logical database** (i.e., the data tables) is closely linked to the physical level, that is, to the underlying files and control system. This close link means a high degree of control over how data is stored and many options for optimizing or speeding up searches.

The close linkage between physical and logical levels also causes a lack of portability. Hierarchical databases only run on particular combinations of hardware and operating systems.

There have been several attempts to separate the physical and logical levels. The CODASYL group designed a database architecture describing the interface between the language in which the tables and the structure were defined and the physical organization of the data. This work first appeared in 1971. Later, the ANSI/SPARC study group produced a standard for network databases. It met some demands for logical data independence, that is, an architecture with a standardized interface between physical and logical levels. It also proposed a standardized interface between the database control systems and the computer.

The idea behind separating the two levels is to allow the user to perform searches and other tasks without considering the machine, storage method or media, or type of pointers used at the physical level. Thus organizations could more easily replace hardware and software to keep up with rapidly changing needs and technology. The emphasis here is on flexibility rather than maximum speed.

1.3 Features

In the late 1960's and early 1970's, workers at the IBM Research Center in San Jose developed a prototype relational database management system called System R. It was the precursor of current IBM products such as SQL/DS and DB2.

In his paper entitled "A Relational Model of Data for Large Shared Data Banks," (*CACM*, Vol. 13 No. 6, June 1970), E.F. Codd laid the groundwork for the relational data model. The theory was basically mathematical. It described both a database structure that was an extension of the ANSI/SPARC architecture *and* a language that could operate on the structure.

The idea behind the relational database was to have a structure that was dynamic, flexible, and user-friendly. Users should be able to manage information without writing programs. The base architecture, like the ANSI/SPARC architecture, featured a sharp separation between physical and logical levels. This was necessary so the user and the database control system could focus on the data. It left the administration of pointers and the physical organization of the database to other agents. Chapter 11 treats this point in more detail.

The structure of the relational database, like that of its predecessors, consists of tables. But there are now two new requirements:

- The database structure must consist of tables **and nothing but tables**. The structure must be "flat" in the sense that only the **contents** of the tables determine which searches or changes are possible. In other words, the structure does not provide for physical arrangements, pointer structures, or other hardware-related elements.

- Definition and manipulation must be **independent** of the physical storage structure. The relational database model thus is a **logical** structure. Its description should have no connection with its physical implementation. The idea is to allow for updating, portability, and distribution.

The database itself should have its own control system, a relational database management system or RDBMS, the operation of which depends on the logical structure alone. As pointers no longer determine which searches are possible, and only the data contents matter, the database control system requires extensions. The solution is the formation of a "data dictionary" or "system catalog". It is a database containing an overview of the original database's structure, that is, for example, specifications of its tables, fields, data types, and indexes. The data dictionary is like a summary of a long report or the table of contents of a book.

The relational DBMS alone determines, based on a logical specification of the database, **how** to find data. The system establishes and maintains "mappings" or "protocols" describing the connections among the DBMS' view of data (in the form of tables), the data dictionary, the physically stored data, and the computer's operating system. The RDBMS can maintain relationships between the logical and physical databases in procedures that in principle should be independent of both levels.

After the DBMS evaluates a command and determines a possible search path through the tables, it calls the mappings. They then call the OS's I/O routines and allow them to fetch the physical data.

The separation of physical and logical aspects means that the DBMS handles all security-related matters, as well as integrity and consistency (for example, keeping two people from updating the same data at the same time). Furthermore, the DBMS itself interprets a search, **finds** an optimal path via tables, and communicates with the mapping procedures.

The fact that the DBMS must analyze each search has limited the acceptance of relational databases in practical applications. "Look before you leap," is a good maxim, but can slow operations drastically. Many early relational databases were simply too slow. The extra analysis and translation takes time and increases system complexity. Only recently have relational DBMSs become fast enough to make their flexibility truly advantageous.

1.4 SQL

Besides defining the logical structure of a database, Codd also defined a relational query language. By 1976, this language had evolved into IBM's SQL (Structured Query Language).

In 1986, ANSI (the American National Standards Institute) published an SQL standard, X3.153. It has led to the development of SQL interfaces for several non-relational databases. Committee work continues to improve and extend the SQL standard and to permit interoperability (through the SQL Access Group). For more information, see C.J. Date, *A Guide to the SQL Standard*, 2nd ed. (Reading, MA: Addison-Wesley, 1989).

1.5 Implementations

In 1979, Oracle Corporation released the first **commercial** relational database, Oracle Version 1.

IBM continued to develop System R, eventually leading to two commercial software products. They are SQL/DS (for 9370 machines and the VM/CMS operating system), which appeared in 1982, and DB2 (designed for large 3090 machines with the MVS operating system), which appeared in 1985.

As opposed to IBM which implemented its products (DB2 and SQL/DS) exclusively on its own mainframes, Oracle developed products for a variety of machines and operating systems. The company first designed software for use on IBM mainframes and DEC computers, but later made the product available for almost every computer and operating system, including MVS and VM. Oracle also developed versions for UNIX, MS-DOS, and OS/2. A common denominator in IBM's and Oracle's products is their use of SQL as the query language. And since SQL is both an ANSI and an ISO standard, it has become a commercial standard for relational database languages.

This book uses SQL/DS and Oracle as examples. The two products have evolved similarly, leading to similar kernels (the basic syntax for table creation and data manipulation). We will focus on this SQL kernel. But SQL/DS and Oracle differ and, in fact, represent two "dialects" of SQL. We will describe standard SQL, but will also discuss how implementations differ.

1.6 Definitions

A database is a group of data items organized for a well-defined purpose. It could, for example, be inventory control, personnel (human resources) management, customer service, payroll, project management, or manufacturing planning in a company. It could also be travel bureau or airline booking, hospital management, or medical or legal record keeping. Any size or type of organization can benefit from having data organized in a database.

A relational database is "a database which appears to the user as a collection of tables (and nothing else)" (Date, *Introduction to Database Systems, Vol. 1,* 5th ed., Addison-Wesley, Reading, MA. 1990). The definition does not state that tables have special relationships, but they are an important aspect of working with databases.

We emphasize "appears to the user", because it reflects the separation between the logical structure and physical storage. Regardless of how the data is stored, it always appears to the user as *tables*. The relational database is a **logical** structure. That is, when a user works with a relational database via SQL, the data appears to be physically stored in a table structure. In fact, of course, it is stored bit by bit on the storage medium and not as tables at all.

Figure 1-2 shows an example of a (logical) table. It consists of three **columns** with the headings "NAME", "AGE", and "SEX". The three headings are variable names. Each variable can, as is apparent, contain many **occurrences** (in this case, five) of the same type of data. The **structure** of the table defines the names and types of the variables that form it.

A column is often called a *field*. In Figure 1-2, the values 33, 23, 44, 12, and 33 are occurrences of the field "AGE", and John Smith is an occurrence of the field "NAME".

The rows of combined fields (i.e., occurrences) form units called *records*. The number of records in a table varies with time; the number at a given moment is the table's *cardinality*.

NAME	AGE	SEX
John Smith	33	M
Ursula Peters	23	F
Morton Berger	44	M
Peter Olson	12	M
Nina Hagen	33	F

Figure 1-2. Example table.

A single record defines a given real-world element, such as the person characterized by name="John Smith", age="33", and sex="M". After all, what is a modern person other than the sum of the data computers keep about him or her? The collection of records defines a type or entity identified by the name of the table. In this case, it might be "Employees".

As with all database structures, there are rules to which a relational table structure must adhere. The following ones are particularly important.

- Field names must be **unique**. In other words, a table may not contain two fields with the same name.

  The reason for this requirement is obvious. A search such as "Find the names of all men in the table" would not work if there were two "sex" fields. Even in a time of sex change operations, one must be able to distinguish the fields, if not their owners.

- The order of the fields cannot matter. We cannot say: "Display column 2." This requirement is closely related to the fact that the relational database is a logical structure. There is, of course, no assurance that all DBAs will put "age" in field 2. Furthermore, there is nothing to prevent a DBA from removing or interchanging columns or inserting new ones in the table structure. A search definition such as: "Select all occurrences from column 2, where column 3='M'" is meaningless. We must refer to fields by name.

- At least one field or **combination** of fields must identify a record **uniquely**. That is, there cannot be two identical records. In Figure 1-2, "name" provides the unique identification.

  In practice, a person's last name is not a good choice for identifying records, since the table could surely include two people with the same last name (such as Bohuslaw

Miropowicz and Stanislaw Miropowicz, or even John Smith and Fred Smith). The requirement states only that at least one combination of field values must be unique for each record. For example, one could combine "name" and "age" to obtain a unique ID. The probability of finding two people with the same name and the same age would be small, although not zero. To keep such coincidences from causing problems, we often introduce an artificial column that insures the uniqueness of each record. It can, for example, contain a consecutive numbering system (employee numbers), a social security number, an account number, or some other identification code. The extra column is not of interest on its own; it is useful only for identification purposes.

Several unique identifications may exist for records in the same table. They may, for example, be an internal number, a social security number, a combination of telephone number and name, or a combination of all fields in the record. Note that at least one such identification must exist or the table would contain identical records.

The unique identification (a field or a combination of fields) is called the **primary key**. If a table has several unique identifiers, they are all candidates for the role of primary key. We therefore refer to them as "candidate keys". We select one and give it the special role of primary key.

We can thus state the requirements as meaning that a table must always have a primary key.

- The order of the individual records cannot matter. The arguments leading to this requirement resemble the ones regarding the order of fields. Again, the issues are flexibility and the physical and logical independence of the data in the relational table. It must be possible to insert and remove records without affecting later operations and applications.

- All fields must be "atomic", i.e., they may not contain multiple values of the same type or meaning. It would, for example, be a **non**-atomic occurrence of field data if one tried to record two bank account balances (such as checking and savings) for someone in the same field. Each must have its own field.

To summarize the five requirements, a database is a collection of uniquely defined tables consisting of a time-varying number of uniquely identifiable occurrences of atomic fields. Although correct, this definition sounds either like something that will blow up the civilized world, or like the report of a committee sent to investigate some unsolvable social or environmental problem.

1.7 Major Example Database

Throughout this book, we will refer to one major example database. We shall therefore describe it briefly here. It describes a company that has its entire operations (for reasons beyond the author's comprehension) in New York state. The firm sells sportswear to clubs, schools, retailers, exercise studios, and other customers. It has salespeople throughout the state who only occasionally come to headquarters for inspirational meetings. They have no affiliation with any company departments.

The main office does all administration and keeps all the inventory.

Employees receive a monthly salary (base pay), plus a commission on sales.

The main office handles all computer needs and keeps centralized databases of customers, employees, orders, and inventory. Individual departments each have a terminal linked to the main system.

The network allows departments to fetch information from the central database for their own local use or processing.

The system is thus highly centralized. More distribution is under consideration to handle future growth and new applications.

The main office keeps the following information in its database (Figure 1-3):

Employee data	Name, address, telephone number, date hired, department, base pay, and type (Dealer, Manager, or Salesperson)
Customer data	Name, address, telephone number, and type (Club, Exercise studio, Retailer, or School)
Order data	Date received, date shipped, items ordered, number ordered, and salesperson
Inventory data	Item names, prices, numbers in stock, and order levels

Note that the zip_code table has only city information as the company's activities are (for obscure regulatory reasons) limited to a single state.

Employees	Customers	Orders
Employee_no	Customer_no	Order_no
First_name	Company_name	Customer_no
Last_name	Street	Employee_no
Street	Zip_code	Received
Zip_code	Telephone	Shipped
Telephone	Type	
Date_hired		
Type		
Department		
Base_pay		

Order_specs	Inventory	Zip_codes
Order_no	Item_no	Zip_code
Item_no	Item_name	City
Quantity	Quantity	
	Price	
	Order_level	

Figure 1-3. Example table structure.

For now, we will not discuss the reasons for choosing the tables and fields. Appendix A specifies the contents of the database in detail.

2

Data Definition

A table is characterized by a name and a set of data elements. Each element has a name and a type specification. This chapter first describes the various types of data elements. It then covers SQL's facilities for defining and changing table structures. Final sections briefly discuss SQL comments and synonyms.

17

2.1 Data Types

When defining a table structure, you must specify the types of the individual data elements. Table 2-1 lists the most common types with typical (system-dependent) ranges.

Table 2-1. Common SQL Data Types

CHAR	Indicated with a specified length. For example, "name CHAR(25)" means that the variable "name" may consist of up to 25 characters. The default length (no specification) is 1. The maximum length is usually about 250. CHARACTER is a synonym in most implementations.
SMALLINT	An integer variable in the range -32,768 to +32,767 (two bytes).
INTEGER	An integer variable in the range -2,147,483,648 to +2,147,483,647 (four bytes).
DECIMAL	Specified with the syntax DECIMAL[(p[,s])] or DEC[(p[,s])], where p (precision) is the number of significant digits and is between 1 and 15. s (scale) is the number cf decimal places and can have any value from 0 to 15-p. Typical examples are DEC(15,0), DEC(7,2), or DEC(0,15). The default, with neither p nor s specified, corresponds to DECIMAL(5.0).
FLOAT	A real number with an absolute value in the range 10^{-308} to 10^{+308} (eight bytes).

We have taken the names of the numeric data types from SQL/DS. Oracle recognizes the specified types and names (for example, when doing conversions), but it operates only with the type NUMBER or NUMBER[(p[,s])]. NUMBER includes the data types mentioned above. When FLOAT is used, NUMBER has the value range -1E128 to +1E128, and INT and DEC have precision p in the range 1<p<38. The ANSI standard also supports the numeric variable types REAL and DOUBLE PRECISION.

The only string type in the ANSI standard is CHAR. Most implementations also have the type VARCHAR, defined as follows:

VARCHAR   CHAR with VARiable length. It is specified as CHAR with a maximum length, as in

```
remark VARCHAR(1000)
```

A variable of type VARCHAR can contain up to 32,767 characters (in SQL/DS) or 65,535 characters (in Oracle, where it is called LONG). During storage of a VARCHAR item, the DBMS reserves only the current length of the string. If the length increases, the rest is stored elsewhere and reached via a pointer.

There are restrictions on VARCHAR variables. You cannot index with them or use them as cluster columns. However, you can perform a search based on them.

The types DATE, TIME, and TIMESTAMP are also available. The first two are subsets of the last. Its value consists of the year, month, day, hour, minute, second, and fraction of a second. The exact format (for example, JAN. 25 1990, 25.01.90) depends on the local implementation (SQL/DS) or some other specified format (Oracle).

Only SQL/DS supports the data types GRAPHIC, VAR-GRAPHIC, and LONG VARGRAPHIC. They are stored as double bytes. Oracle supports the comparable data types RAW and LONG RAW for binary data.

2.2 Defining Table Structures

The **Data Definition Language** (or DDL) is used to create, alter, and delete table **structures**. A table structure is defined in terms of individual elements (fields). A field is identified by a name, a type, and possibly an additional specification.

The general syntax for defining a table is:

```
CREATE TABLE table_name
(field_name field_type [NOT NULL]
[{,field_name field_type [NOT NULL]}]...)
```

Appendix B explains the notation. We read the above statement as follows. The **command** is CREATE TABLE, a reserved word. Next comes the table's name. Then comes a left parenthesis, followed by the first variable's name and type. An option is to specify the field as NOT NULL, meaning that it cannot be left empty. The default is NULL, meaning that the field can be empty.

Subsequent fields (which are optional) have the same specification. Commas separate fields, and a right parenthesis ends the definition. SQL/DS restricts table names and field names to 14 characters, in accordance with ANSI recommendations. Oracle allows up to 30. A table may contain up to 254 fields.

Figures 2-1 and 2-2 show the definition of tables called "employees" and "orders", respectively. Note that we show commands, types, and options in uppercase, names in lowercase.

```
CREATE TABLE employees
(employee_no INTEGER NOT NULL,
first_name CHAR(20),
last_name CHAR(25),
street CHAR(30),
zip_code CHAR(5),
date_hired DATE,
type CHAR(1))
```

Figure 2-1. Definition of employee table.

```
CREATE TABLE orders
(order_no INTEGER NOT NULL,
customer_no INTEGER NOT NULL,
employee_no INTEGER,
received DATE NOT NULL,
shipped DATE)
```

Figure 2-2. Definition of order table.

The table names must be unique within the database, and the field names must be unique within a table. A system-assigned user ID identifies the table's creator. This information is part of the data dictionary or system catalog (see Chapter 6).

We have specified some fields as NOT NULL. In the order case, this prevents a user from entering a record without an order number, customer number, or date received. In the employee case, it prevents a user from entering a record without an employee number. Obviously, a table's primary key must be NOT NULL, as we would have no way of finding records with null entries. NOT NULL is a necessary but not sufficient condition for a primary key, as its values must be unique as well as non-null. All other fields could be empty, due to the information being either nonexistent or unavailable.

To remove a table, use the command

```
DROP TABLE table_name
```

As mentioned previously, a relational database consists exclusively of tables. A table is usually not stored in its own individual file. In practice, database programs such as SQL/DS and Oracle do not severely restrict the number of tables per database (SQL/DS has an upper limit of 8 million tables!). Thus a database may consist of 100 tables, which could be stored in one data file. Therefore, database programs cannot deal with tables by file name. Instead, the user must define units called **dataspaces** and indicate which one to use in each table definition. The form is:

```
CREATE TABLE test768
(field definitions)
SPACE my_example_tables
```

If you do not indicate a SPACE, the database system will automatically use a default one. The dataspace concept is very important in relational databases as a way to emphasize logical and physical data independence.

2.3 Changing Table Structures

Sometimes, new requirements or misjudgments mean that we must revise a table's structure. Relational database management systems allow some changes (the most common in practice) to be made easily. For example, we can readily add fields. Deleting fields or altering their definitions is much more difficult, but fortunately much less often needed.

We can add new field definitions to a table using the command sequence:

```
ALTER TABLE table_name
ADD field_name type [{,field_name type}]...
```

For example, we can add the new fields middle_name and age to the employees table with the command:

```
ALTER TABLE employees
ADD middle_name CHAR(11), age SMALLINT
```

Both Oracle and SQL/DS allow users to ADD fields. They also expand existing records to contain the new fields. We cannot usually specify the new fields as NOT NULL because their contents in existing records will be NULL. In Oracle, however, you can specify NOT NULL and change a field's length and data type, as long as the table is empty.

When dealing with non-empty tables, you must perform an intermediate step. Create a temporary table into which you may move the data while altering the original (Oracle) or creating a completely new one with the correct definitions (SQL/DS). Afterward, you can move the data back. For example, in Oracle we can expand the first_name field in the employees table to 30 characters with:

```
ALTER TABLE employees
MODIFY (first_name CHAR(30) NOT NULL)
```

However, be careful! Problems can occur if you return values to fields defined as NOT NULL, string fields that have changed length, or fields that have changed type. In Oracle, we can change a table's name (RENAME old_table_name TO new_table_name), but not in SQL/DS. Renaming tables is risky, as the names are often used elsewhere (in views and applications). Changing names can thus cause programs to fail.

Removing a field from a definition is not easy. The problem is that one does not know where the removal might cause problems, such as in other tables, programs, or view definitions. However, see Section 3.3 for a possible solution.

2.4 Comments

As a table owner or a DBA, you can insert comments about tables or columns. The ANSI standard does not cover comments, but the following syntax is common to both Oracle and SQL/DS.

```
COMMENT ON
{TABLE table_name | COLUMN table_name.column_name}
IS 'string'
```

To add a comment to field order_no in table "orders", use either of the following commands.

```
COMMENT ON TABLE orders
IS 'the relationships among customers, orders, and
employees'
```

```
COMMENT ON COLUMN orders.order_no
IS 'unique determination of a particular order'
```

Comments on columns and tables appear in the tables of the system catalog (see Chapter 6). You can see their text by making an inquiry.

2.5 Synonyms

Table names are often long (to be reasonable descriptive or mnemonic), and referring to them frequently is inconvenient and error-prone. The problem is worse if you are working with other people's tables, because then you must enter the owner's name as well as the table's. One solution is to introduce abbreviations or **synonyms** using the command:

```
CREATE SYNONYM synonym
FOR owner_of_table.table_name
```

Only the person who executes the command can use the synonym. However, as noted, it can apply to tables created by someone else. If Jones has created a table named telephone_list, you can establish the synonym tls for it as follows:

```
CREATE SYNONYM tls
FOR jones.telephone_list
```

You can refer to the table later as either tls or jones.telephone_list.

Synonyms are recorded in a system catalog table. Note that removing a table does not automatically delete them. You must remove them explicitly using the command

```
DROP SYNONYM synonym
```

In Oracle, the DBA can also specify the synonym **type** as PUBLIC (CREATE PUBLIC SYNONYM synonym FOR table_name). All users can access a PUBLIC synonym.

3

Data Manipulation

The **data manipulation language** (DML) handles operations such as entering records into a table, changing data, deleting records, and extracting data from records and tables. With DML, one does not change the table's **structure**, but rather its **contents**.

The DML commands are:

DELETE   removes records from a table

INSERT   enters records into a table

SELECT   extracts data from records in a table

UPDATE   changes the values of the fields in a record

INSERT is the essential command for entering data into the database.

DELETE is the opposite of INSERT. You use it to remove records from a table, either all of them or just ones satisfying certain criteria. Note that you cannot use DELETE to delete the table or its structure.

With the UPDATE command, you can alter existing records. You can change either an entire column or individual records that satisfy specified conditions. UPDATE thus lets you clear or blank records but not delete them or change their structure.

SELECT is the most comprehensive DML command. It has several functions, but the most common is to extract data from a table. You can also use SELECT to restrict the coverage of INSERT, UPDATE, or DELETE.

For printing data, most DBMSs have built-in functions and report formatting commands. Many vendors also provide add-on report writers.

3.1 Conditions

A common characteristic of UPDATE, DELETE, and SELECT is that the user can specify **conditions**. We must therefore discuss conditions, and the arithmetic, logical, and relational operators used to form them.

Conditions are an important aspect of data manipulation. They consist of logical (boolean) **expressions** that are either true or false. A typical example is

```
customer_no > 200 or item_name = "ball"
```

It is true if either part is true (or both), and false otherwise.

Fields with the value NULL have a special status. Conditions involving them are neither true nor false, only "unknown". That is, we know nothing about NULL values. After all, they typically are empty fields about which we have no information.

We can formulate a typical search with a condition as follows:

```
SELECT *
FROM employees
WHERE employee_no = 22
```

The command selects all fields (indicated by the asterisk) in the employee table from records for which employee_no = 22.

The condition is preceded by the word WHERE. Then we have the expression itself, which must be either true or false. The computer examines each record in the employee table to determine whether employee_no is 22. If the search returns true, the computer prints the record's data values. Otherwise, it proceeds to the next record.

A condition can be **compound**. That is, it can consist of expressions joined using logical operators, such as AND, OR, or XOR. The overall logical expression is either true or false.

AND and OR have the same meanings as in normal English speech. The compound condition expression_1 AND expression_2 is true if **both** expression_1 **and** expression_2 are true. The compound condition expression_1 OR expression_2 is true if **either** expression_1 **or** expression_2 (or both) is true. AND takes priority over OR, so the computer evaluates ANDs first.

Some implementations also provide the less common logical operator XOR or exclusive OR (either but not both). The compound condition expression_1 XOR expression_2 is true if **either** expression_1 **or** expression_2 is true, but false if both are true.

Consider the following example of a compound expression:

```
SELECT * FROM employees
WHERE type = 'M'
AND zip_code = '14031'
```

The statement has the following effect: Print all records in the employees table that have type M and zip_code 14031.

To find all managers (type M) who reside in either Zip Code 14031 **or** 14150, we must use parentheses. The correct statement is:

```
SELECT * FROM employees
WHERE type = 'M' AND (zip_code = '14031' OR zip_code =
'14150')
```

Without the parentheses, the computer would do the AND first. It would thus find managers living in Zip Code 14031, but it would report everyone living in Zip Code 14150. Do you see why? Parentheses change the normal order of operations. The computer evaluates everything inside them before what is outside.

Expressions need not be simple field variables or constants. They can also be the results of calculations based on fields. If, for example, you want to print a list of items that have an inventory level within 10% of the order level, you can use the statement:

```
SELECT * FROM inventory
WHERE quantity < order_level * 1.1
```

Do not confuse the * after SELECT (meaning "all fields") with the multiplication operator *. Unfortunately, there are not enough special characters on standard keyboards to avoid such double meanings.

The computer evaluates arithmetic expressions according to operator priority. * and / have higher priority than + and -, so it does them first. When dealing with operators that have the same priority (such as * and /, and + and -), it works from left to right. As noted earlier, the computer evaluates terms inside parentheses before ones outside them. The same order applies within parentheses if there are multiple levels.

The following relational operators have the same priority:

=	**Equal to**. An expression is true if the two sides are equal.
>	**Greater than**. An expression is true if the left side is larger than the right side. For string expressions (such as "Smythe">"Smith"), the ASCII values determine the string values.
<	**Less than**. An expression is true if the left side is less than the right side. For string expressions (such as "Smythe"<"Smith"), the ASCII values determine the string values.
< >	**Not equal to**. An expression is true if the two sides are not equal. For string expressions (such as "Smythe"< >"Smith"), the ASCII

values determine the string values. Some implementations allow (as in C) != or ^= instead of < >.

>=	Greater than or equal to.
<=	Less than or equal to.
IN	Equal to an element of. …WHERE last_name IN ('Smith','Smythe'). The expression is true if last_name is either "Smith" or "Smythe". …WHERE employee_no IN (12,23,45,56). The expression is true if the employee number is 12, 23, 45, or 56.
BETWEEN…AND	The expression is true if the left value lies in the inclusive interval specified by BETWEEN and AND. …WHERE employee_no BETWEEN 23 AND 28. The expression is true if employee_no is between 23 and 28 inclusive. …WHERE last_name BETWEEN 'Chris' AND 'Christopher'. The expression is true if last_name is between Chris and Christopher alphabetically.
EXISTS	Used only with subqueries (see more about them later in the chapter.) The expression is true if a subquery returns at least one record. …WHERE EXISTS (SELECT * FROM employees WHERE zip_code = '14031') The expression is true if there is at least one employee living in Zip Code 14031.

ALL/ANY/SOME	Used only with subqueries. Please see examples later (SOME is a synonym for ANY).
LIKE	Used in pattern matching. ...WHERE last_name LIKE '%mer'. True for Cramer, Craemer, Kraemer, Kramer, or Kremer, i.e., all names ending in "mer". ...WHERE last_name LIKE 'Nels%'. True for Nelsen, Nelson, or Nelsson, i.e., names beginning with "Nels". ...WHERE last_name LIKE 'ar_y'. True for Carey, Caray, Karey, and Karay, i.e., for last names of the form "_ar_y". The underscore indicates a variable (any character).
IS NULL	Used in searches to determine whether a field contains a value. The search returns true if the field is empty and false if it is not. ...WHERE first_name IS NULL ...WHERE department IS NOT NULL Note that a null field is not equal to anything, not even another null field.

The following logical operations have lower priority than the above:

AND	True if both expressions are true. The computer evaluates AND before OR.
NOT	NOT "inverts" the truth value of a logical expression. ...WHERE NOT (employee_no > 34) is equivalent to ...WHERE employee_no <= 34.

...WHERE last_name NOT IN ('Smith','Smythe') True for any name except Smith or Smythe. NOT IN means "different from all elements in".
The computer evaluates NOT before AND, OR, and XOR.

OR

True if one or both of the expressions are true.

XOR

True if one expression is true, but not both. Not part of the ANSI standard.

3.2 SELECT

The SELECT command extracts data from a table. The result is always a new temporary table (a *result table*). It can be displayed, printed, stored on disk, or sent to another table.

The syntax for the SELECT command is:

```
SELECT [DISTINCT] [*|field_name {,field_name}...]
FROM table_name [{,table_name}...]
[WHERE condition]
[[GROUP BY grouping_criteria] [HAVING predicate]]
[ORDER BY ordering_criteria]
```

The simplest possible SELECT applied to the customer table would be:

```
SELECT *
FROM customers
```

The asterisk, as usual, means "all fields". The computer prints the entire table as the result table. The records appear in the order in which they were entered.

```
SELECT * FROM inventory;
```

ITEM_NO	ITEM_NAME	QUANTITY	PRICE	ORDER_LEVEL
4012	Caddies	2	120	1
4013	Golf balls	545	2	250
4014	Flags (golf)	180	5	48
4017	Green clipper	20	4.4	15

To print only certain fields, specify them in the printout list. The computer prints them in the order you name them. For example, to list customer_no, company_name, and type for all records in the customer table, use the following command. Only part of the result table appears here.

```
SELECT company_name, customer_no, type FROM customers;
```

COMPANY_NAME	CUSTOMER_NO	TYPE
South Ball Club	1001	C
East Side Club	1002	C
Lehigh High School	1003	S
Jack's Exercise Studio	1004	E

This shows how to print a subset of the columns of a table. If, on the other hand, you want to print a subset of the records, you must introduce conditions.

To print customer_no, company_name, telephone, and type for all clubs (type C) in the customer table, enter:

```
SELECT customer_no,company_name,telephone,type
FROM customers
WHERE type = 'C';
```

CUSTOMER_NO	COMPANY_NAME	TELEPHONE	TYPE
1001	South Ball Club	327-5432	C
1002	East Side Club	339-8070	C

You can combine conditions as in the following search. Let us find the customer_no, company_name, telephone, and type of all clubs in Zip Code 14031:

```
SELECT customer_no,company_name,telephone,type
FROM customers
WHERE zip_code = '14031' AND type = 'C';
```

CUSTOMER_NO	COMPANY_NAME	TELEPHONE	TYPE
1001	South Ball Club	327-5432	C

In many practical situations, you do not have a precise description of the values you want. For example, suppose you want to list all inventory items for handball players. You cannot simply pose the condition WHERE item_name='handball'. Instead you must look for a substring using a LIKE predicate.

```
SELECT item_name, price, price *.10 "SALES TAX", price
*1.10 "NET PRICE"
```

```
FROM inventory
WHERE item_name LIKE 'Handball%'
```

ITEM_NAME	PRICE	SALES TAX	NET PRICE
Handball net	78.60	7.86	86.46
Handballs (men)	23.10	2.31	25.41
Handballs (women)	32.10	3.21	35.31
Handball goals	234.20	23.42	257.62

Note the following about this search:

- The LIKE clause searches the field "item_name" for all names that **begin** with "Handball". What follows is irrelevant. Note that % means "any character string, including the null string".

- We can do calculations using fields and print the results (as in price * .10 or price * 1.10). The calculated fields have no names in the table, and their column headings will normally just be the computational expressions. In Oracle, you can change the heading by specifying a new name inside quotation marks ("SALES TAX" or "NET PRICE"). In SQL/DS, you must indicate the new column headings in an independent format statement such as:

```
FORMAT column 2 name 'SALES TAX'
```

ORDER BY

The individual records in relational databases are stored in the order in which they were entered. Only by using special methods such as clustering (see Chapter 5) can you change this. Often, however, you want to display selected records in a specific order. The ORDER BY clause does the job.

ORDER BY must be followed by field names whose values indicate the printed order. If several names appear, the ordering will be done first on the basis of the first field. If there are duplicate values, records are ordered according to the second field, and so on. The value of a field is either its ASCII value or its numerical value.

Fields included in the ORDER BY clause can be sorted either with the smallest value first (ASC or ASCENDING) or with the largest first (DESC or DESCENDING). ASC is the default. The next example uses the fields "received" and "shipped" as part of the search key. Both are of type DATE. Many functions are generally available for working with DATE variables. Typical examples include functions for adding or subtracting days, hours, years, or months; finding the latest of two dates; and converting a DATE variable to a CHAR variable. The specific syntax varies with the implementation. The ANSI standard does not mention DATE variables.

```
SELECT customer_no,order_no,received,shipped
FROM orders
WHERE customer_no < 1003
AND received > '01-AUG-89'
AND shipped < '31-AUG-89'
ORDER BY customer_no, order_no DESC
```

CUSTOMER_NO	ORDER_NO	RECEIVED	SHIPPED
1001	2015	23-AUG-89	29-AUG-89
1001	2012	22-AUG-89	28-AUG-89
1001	2004	08-AUG-89	30-AUG-89
1002	2016	25-AUG-89	30-AUG-89
1002	2008	16-AUG-89	24-AUG-89
1002	2001	03-AUG-89	15-AUG-89

Note that the results are listed first by customer number (smallest first), then by order number (largest first because of the DESC specification).

Built-In Functions

SQL includes only simple statistics as standard functions, namely AVG (average), COUNT (number), MAX (maximum), MIN (minimum), and SUM (summation). A typical example of their use is:

```
SELECT MIN(base_pay) "MINIMUM",
MAX(base_pay) "MAXIMUM",
AVG(base_pay) "AVERAGE",
SUM(base_pay) "SUM",
COUNT(base_pay) "NUMBER"
FROM employees
```

MINIMUM	MAXIMUM	AVERAGE	SUM	NUMBER
1200	1800	1575	18900	12

COUNT allows the option (DISTINCT field_name) which counts only different values in the field.

You can combine functions in a compound expression such as

```
SELECT MAX(base_pay) - AVG(base_pay)
```

There are, however, restrictions on using the built-in functions. They arise from the fact that a function can return only one value. Thus, you cannot issue statements like

```
SELECT first_name, MAX(base_pay)
```

MAX (base_pay) is a single number, whereas first_name is an entire column. To find employees who earn the maximum base pay, you must select records based on a condition.

As mentioned, only simple functions are built-in. To compute more complex expressions, you must work in an ordinary programming language (see Chapter 9 on embedded SQL).

GROUP BY and HAVING

The GROUP BY clause lets you group the results of a SELECT command before printing them. For example, to print the number of orders placed by individual customers, you can issue the following search command.

```
SELECT COUNT(*), customer_no
FROM orders
GROUP BY customer_no
ORDER BY COUNT(*);
```

COUNT(*)	CUSTOMER_NO
1	1005
1	1006
2	1004
3	1001
4	1002
4	1003

Note that the fields used in GROUP BY must appear in the print-out list. However, you can apply the built-in statistical functions (such as COUNT) to create an expression for grouping. Consider the following example. We want to determine the number of employees and average wages in each department. The report covers only employees who were hired after January 1, 1975, and only departments where the average monthly wage exceeds $1600.

```
SELECT department, AVG(base_pay), COUNT(*)
FROM employees
WHERE date_hired > '01-JAN-75'
GROUP BY department
HAVING AVG(base_pay) > 1600
```

DEPT	AVG(BASE_PAY)	COUNT(*)
A20	1680	5
A30	1725	2
A40	1725	2

Note the use of the HAVING clause. It has the same effect with GROUP BY as WHERE does on individual records. WHERE and HAVING can appear together in a statement. The example works as follows:

1. Select all employees who were hired after January 1, 1975.

2. Group the selected records by department.

3. Select only groups (departments) where the average base pay exceeds $1600.

4. Print the name of the department, the average base pay for the group, and the number of members.

The GROUP BY predicate (department) *must* appear in the printout list.

Subqueries

Sometimes, we want to use a SELECT statement within a WHERE clause. The SELECT thus forms part of the condition. We refer to such a query within a query as a **subquery** or **nested** SELECT statement. The provision for subqueries is the basis for referring to SQL as a "structured" language.

Some searches are impossible to do without subqueries. You can also use them to control how the DBMS performs the search or to clarify precisely what you want done.

You must enclose subqueries inside parentheses. As in other situations involving parentheses, the computer executes everything within the innermost ones first. Thus it does the subquery before the overall query, just as you would expect. The computer returns the values from the nested (innermost) SELECT to the surrounding one.

A simple example of a subquery is the following. Suppose you want to list everyone who works in the same department as employee 33. Perhaps he or she is being considered for a promotion or is being investigated for criminal activity, security violations, or expense account padding. Here the subquery must determine the department id that we will then use in the query.

```
SELECT employee_no,last_name
FROM employees
WHERE department =
(SELECT department FROM employees
WHERE employee_no = 33)
```

EMPLOYEE_NO	LAST_NAME
33	Gilbert
18	Smith
19	Larimer
27	Madison
56	Olson

We could add

```
ORDER BY last_name
```

or

```
ORDER BY employee_no
```

to order the results.

The computer evaluates the expression inside parentheses first. It returns the department number for employee 33 and transfers it to the surrounding query. That query then operates as usual. The rule that parentheses determine the priority of operations applies here.

In the next example, we want to determine who earns the most money in the company. Perhaps we need the information to comply with government reporting requirements or to identify who should be laid off in the next cutback. Here we use a subquery to find all employees who earn the maximum pay. Remember, there could be many such people, so we cannot just apply MAX by itself. Instead, we allow the innermost parentheses to report the maximum base pay. The main query can then use that value in its search.

```
SELECT first_name, last_name, base_pay
FROM employees
WHERE base_pay =
(SELECT MAX(base_pay)
FROM employees);
```

FIRST_NAME	LAST_NAME	BASE_PAY
Paul	Gilbert	1800
Norman	Peterson	1800
Ursula	Klein	1800

If a subquery could return multiple values, you can apply only the IN operator to its result. Consider, for example, the following search operation, where the object is to find employees who were the first to be hired in each department. Perhaps we want to honor them or see if we are complying with special seniority rules. The subquery must return a date for each department. Thus, it must include a GROUP BY department clause.

```
SELECT department, first_name, last_name, date_hired
FROM employees
WHERE date_hired IN
   (SELECT MIN(date_hired)
```

```
   FROM employees
   GROUP BY department)
ORDER BY department
```

DEPT	FIRST_NAME	LAST_NAME	DATE_HIRED
	Ivan	Jacobs	25-JUN-86
A20	Michael	Olson	12-JUN-85
A30	Ursula	Klein	01-JAN-86
A40	Norman	Peterson	01-JAN-86

Searches Involving Several Tables

A database usually consists of many tables. Together they define the information resources of a company or organization. The division into individual tables is a major design decision. Some designs, of course, are more functional and operate more efficiently than others. A good design must allow for the associations that exist in the actual data.

For example, customers may place many orders, each involving many items. Thus we must connect the customer table with the order table, and the order table with the inventory table. The connections are important, as they allow us to report a customer's order history, the current stock of items ordered by a particular customer, the list of customers who have ordered a particular item, or the list of orders involving a particular item.

If you examine the description of our example tables (Figure 1-3 in Chapter 1), you can see that some fields appear several times. The customer, order, and order_specs tables all have the field customer_no. The order_specs and inventory tables both contain the field item_no. We call such fields "join predicates" because they join or link tables.

Thus, if one knows customer_no, one can find the customer's orders by using the join predicate in a condition to form a so-called "natural join" of the two tables (sometimes also called "register cross referencing"). If one knows the item_no in an order_specs record, one can find the item_name and price in the inventory. Fields that form join predicates need not have the same name, but must (naturally!) be of the same type. Of course, they must also have the same **meaning**. For example, we can use the following command to list the orders for each customer. We obtain the company name from the customer table and the order number from the order table. The listing below shows only part of the result.

```
SELECT customers.company_name, orders.order_no
FROM customers, orders
WHERE customers.customer_no = orders.customer_no
```

COMPANY_NAME	ORDER_NO
South Ball Club	2004
South Ball Club	2015
South Ball Club	2012
Jack's Exercise Studio	2001
Jack's Exercise Studio	2008

When cross-referencing tables, we can use the join predicate. Here we used an "equijoin", because we were seeking *equality* between the predicate values. The search causes the DBMS to scan the customer table first (because it is the smallest) and find the first customer_no. It then uses that number to search all records in the order table. Each time it finds one with the given customer_no, it collects the data from it, along with data from the record in the customer table. Finally, it prints the result table.

Besides specifying the join predicate, we must also specify all tables to be used in the FROM clause. The order is immaterial.

As mentioned earlier, field names need not be unique within a database, although they must be unique within a table. In practice, fields in different tables often have the same names. This is particularly true of join predicates. For the DBMS to know which fields are of interest, we must qualify ambiguous names with their table name. One qualifies a field by putting the table name ahead of the field name with a period in-between, as shown in the next example.

If you use a long, descriptive table name, you can specify a **temporary** synonym for it (also called a *correlation name*) in a FROM clause as in:

```
SELECT e.employee_no, first_name, last_name, order_no
FROM orders o, employees e
WHERE e.employee_no = o.employee_no;
```

Note that the DBMS applies the FROM statement first. Hence we can use the synonyms in both the printout list (even though it appears before the FROM) and the WHERE condition. Obviously, typing e and o is far more convenient and less error-prone than repeatedly typing "employees" and "orders". The advantage is even greater for table names that also involve an owner, such as central.employees.

A temporary synonym applies only to the current command. To make it permanent, issue the command

```
CREATE SYNONYM synonym FOR owner_of_the_table table_name
```

A search can involve more than two tables. The next search determines the total purchases made by Lehigh High School. The report must print item names, quantities, prices, and total costs. So the

DBMS must obtain the customer number from the customer table, the corresponding order numbers from the order table, the item quantities from the order_specs table, and the prices from the inventory table. We have numbered the lines for later reference.

```
1   SELECT i.item_name, os.quantity, i.price,
2   os.quantity * i.price "TOTAL"
3   FROM customers c, orders o, order_specs os,
       inventory i
4   WHERE c.customer_no = o.customer_no
5   AND o.order_no = os.order_no
6   AND os.item_no = i.item_no
7   AND c.company_name = 'Lehigh High School'
8   ORDER BY o.order_no
```

ITEM_NAME	QUANTITY	PRICE	TOTAL
Soccer ball	2	43.7	87.4
Skipping rope (10 ft.)	30	2.2	66.0
Skipping rope (8 ft.)	30	1.7	51.0
Volleyball	3	20.0	60.0
Handballs (women's)	3	32.1	96.3
Skipping rope (10 ft.)	12	2.2	26.4
Soccer ball	3	43.7	131.1
Tennis balls (white)	17	10.4	176.8
Soccer ball	4	43.7	174.8

The database management system starts with the last condition (c.company_name="Lehigh High School"), as it is the most restrictive. This reduces the number of access keys to the tables.

The concept of **cartesian product** is important here. To illustrate what it means, consider two tables, A and B. Table A consists of two records with field values AA,AB and AC,AD. Table B also consists of two records with field values BA,BB and BC,BD. Figure 3-1 shows the cartesian product. Note that its records have four fields and their values consist of all combinations of the values of A and B.

Table A	Table B	Cartesian product (A X B)
AA AB AC AD	BA BB BC BD	AA AB BA BB AA AB BC BD AC AD BA BB AC AD BC BD

Figure 3-1. Cartesian product of tables A and B.

Let us now describe how the last search proceeds.

Line 7:   The computer finds the record for Lehigh High School in the customer table and determines customer_no.

Line 4:   The search moves to the order table via a join between c.customer_no and o.customer_no. The computer finds all order numbers for Lehigh High School. What we are doing is examining the cartesian product of the customer table and the order table.

Line 5:   The search now moves to the order specification table via a join between o.order_no and os.order_no. The computer finds all records in the order specification table for Lehigh High School. Here we are examining a new cartesian product between the preceding one and the order_specs table.

Line 6:   The search finally moves to the inventory table via a join between os.item_no and i.item_no. The computer finds all records in the inventory table for items ordered by Lehigh High School. Here we are examining the cartesian product between the preceding product and the inventory table.

Thus the computer has essentially formed a cartesian product of all four tables. It does not print the product, but it exists temporarily in memory (and can cause an annoying "Out of Memory" error if the tables are too large!). The computer finally determines the TOTAL field, sorts the report according to the field o.order_no (line 8), and prints the result.

Another search lists departments that received orders for more than 3 items. Here we are looking at our better performers. They may survive the latest merger, layoff, or consolidation.

```
SELECT department, COUNT(*), SUM(price)
FROM employees e, orders o, order_specs os,
    inventory i
WHERE e.employee_no = o.employee_no
AND o.order_no = os.order_no
AND os.item_no = i.item_no
GROUP BY department
HAVING COUNT(*) > 3
AND department IS NOT NULL
```

DEPT	COUNT(*)	SUM(PRICE)
A20	23	724.6
A30	9	222.6
A40	8	356.2

Note that we grouped the combined records using GROUP BY department. HAVING COUNT(*) selects groups according to the number of records. The condition limits the selection to cases in which the number exceeds 3. The requirement that department IS NOT NULL avoids including salespeople who are **not** associated with a particular department. An alternative approach would be to insert AND e.type <> 'S'. Remember that you must use IS with NULL, as null fields are not equal to anything.

Outer Join

A (natural) join combines two tables via fields that contain the same value. They could, for example, be the employee and order tables. But the natural join does not include records that have no matches in the other database. For example, suppose we also want to list employees who have no orders registered. Then we must use a so-called **outer join** that includes non-matching records.

We can formulate the query as follows for employees in department A20:

```
SELECT first_name, last_name, order_no
FROM orders o, employees e
WHERE e.employee_no = o.employee_no(+)
AND department = 'A20'
ORDER BY last_name, order_no
```

FIRST_NAME	LAST_NAME	ORDER_NO
Joan	Smith	
Allan	Larimer	
George	Madison	
Paul	Gilbert	2001
Paul	Gilbert	2002
Paul	Gilbert	2007
Michael	Olson	2008
Michael	Olson	2016
Michael	Olson	2018

We indicate an outer join by putting a plus sign in parentheses after the join predicate that may be NULL. The results include employees with no orders as well as those with some, along with the specific order numbers involved.

Correlated Subqueries

Correlated here means **interacting**. The interaction involves data values sent back and forth between the overall query and the subquery. This special type of search involves just one table, but it uses the ideas derived from linking tables via a join predicate and bases the search on a subquery.

For example, to determine who earns more than the average pay in each department, issue the following correlated subquery.

```
SELECT department, first_name, last_name, base_pay
FROM employees x
WHERE base_pay >
   (SELECT AVG(base_pay)
   FROM employees
```

```
WHERE department = x.department)
ORDER BY department
```

DEPT	FIRST_NAME	LAST_NAME	BASE_PAY
A20	Paul	Gilbert	1800
A30	Ursula	Klein	1800
A40	Norman	Peterson	1800

In correlated subqueries, a table must have two names (here employees and x). The interactive element is that the subquery must first get the number of one department. It uses the number in a condition (WHERE department = x.department) to determine the average base pay for the employee's department. It sends the result back to the overall query which makes a comparison (base_pay>...). Then the subquery fetches the next department number, computes the average, and so on. Finally, the overall query prints the result.

IN Operator

The IN operator checks whether a variable belongs to a set. The result is true if the variable's value is in the set. Otherwise, it is false. IN is thus equivalent to a combination (logical OR) of individual comparisons. For example:

```
SELECT first_name, last_name
FROM employees
WHERE employee_no IN (19, 26, 33)
```

is the same as:

```
SELECT first_name, last_name
FROM employees
WHERE employee_no = 19 OR employee_no = 26
OR employee_no = 33;
```

The statement

```
SELECT first_name, last_name FROM employees
```

is executed if the compound condition is true. The search thus examines individual records in the employee table. If the employee number is in the specified set, it prints the name.

We often use the IN operator when a subquery returns a set of elements. For example, to list all items in the order_specs table, issue the query:

```
SELECT item_name
FROM inventory
WHERE item_no IN
    (SELECT DISTINCT item_no
    FROM order_specs);
```

The subquery (SELECT DISTINCT...) returns a set (a table) consisting of all distinct item numbers from the order_specs table. The WHERE item_no IN clause delivers item numbers one at a time.

To list all items **not** included in any order, simply negate the IN condition. The form is

```
WHERE item_no NOT IN
```

ANY, ALL, and SOME

Suppose you want to use the comparison predicates but your subquery returns a set of values, rather than just one. You must modify the subquery by preceding it with ANY or ALL. SOME is a synonym for ANY. The subquery cannot involve BETWEEN...AND.

A typical search is:

```
SELECT first_name, last_name
FROM employees
WHERE base_pay>ALL
   (SELECT base_pay
   FROM employees
   WHERE department='A30')
```

The result is the names of all employees who earn more than everyone in department A30. ALL essentially selects the highest value returned by the subquery.

If we use ANY or SOME instead of ALL, the result would be the names of all employees who earn more than someone in department A30. That is, all who earn more than the lowest-paid person in the department. Be careful here, as English usage is for "any" to mean "all" or "every", as in "The noise is louder than any I have ever heard". Or, as Cole Porter once put it, "Heaven knows, anything goes." SQL strictly uses ANY to mean "any single occurrence".

EXISTS

EXISTS and NOT EXISTS are used only with subqueries. The following query determines who took orders from customer 1002.

Perhaps the customer wants to deal with the same people again (or never again!), or there has been a mix-up in orders.

```
SELECT employee_no, first_name, last_name
FROM employees e
WHERE EXISTS
    (SELECT * FROM orders o
    WHERE customer_no = 1002
    AND o.employee_no = e.employee_no)
```

EMPLOYEE_NO	FIRST_NAME	LAST_NAME
33	Paul	Gilbert
56	Michael	Olson

The DBMS works by first recording the value of the field employee_no. It then sends the various employee_no's one by one to the subquery. The subquery searches the order table for the employee number. If it finds the number, it returns the corresponding record to the external query, which then prints the result. Thus the use of EXISTS implies that the DBMS does the search *without* considering the priority introduced by parentheses.

We can reformulate searches involving the EXISTS predicate to use IN instead (the reverse is not always true). Thus, the following search yields the same result as its predecessor:

```
SELECT employee_no, first_name, last_name
FROM employees e
WHERE employee_no IN
    (SELECT employee_no
    FROM orders o
    WHERE o.employee_no = e.employee_no
    AND customer_no = 1002)
```

NOT EXISTS is the opposite of EXISTS. It is true if no case satisfies the subquery.

The following search reports on employees, associated with a department, who do not yet have an order from a customer. Perhaps a performance review or a brief tongue-lashing is in order. Here the external search sends employee numbers to the subquery one at a time. If the subquery locates a record, it is returned. But it goes no further because of the NOT EXISTS. Thus the query lists only employees who have no orders recorded.

```
SELECT employee_no, first_name, last_name
FROM employees e
WHERE department IS NOT NULL
AND NOT EXISTS
   (SELECT * FROM orders o
   WHERE o.employee_no = e.employee_no)
ORDER BY employee_no
```

EMPLOYEE_NO	FIRST_NAME	LAST_NAME
14	Peter	Swan
18	Joan	Smith
19	Allan	Larimer
26	Stephanie	Nickels
27	George	Madison

Optimization

Our examples have combined many different records from many different tables. The DBMS automatically optimizes the search based on which tables are indexed, their sizes, which data is already available in buffers, and other factors. However, the user can also do some optimization by using subqueries to force the DBMS to perform searches in a particular order.

The following two searches produce the same result:

```
SELECT first_name, last_name
FROM employees WHERE employee_no IN
    (SELECT employee_no FROM orders
    WHERE customer_no IN
    (SELECT customer_no FROM customers
    WHERE company_name = 'Lehigh High School'))
```

```
SELECT DISTINCT first_name, last_name
FROM employees e,orders o,customers c
WHERE c.customer_no = o.customer_no
AND e.employee_no = o.employee_no
AND company_name = 'Lehigh High School'
```

The first search begins inside the innermost parentheses. Thus the DBMS must search just one table. And because the customer table is relatively small (compared to the order or inventory table), the search requires few disk operations. It produces just a few selected values for the external search to consider. The DBMS (or its optimizer) can then identify the records. The results of the second subquery are the values actually required to perform the external search. In this way, the partial searches yield only records that are essential for further processing.

The second search must examine all possible combinations of c.customer_no and o.customer_no. In principle, i.e., without the DBMS itself doing an optimization, one can say that it must form a cartesian product of tables c and o. Thus it must examine all combinations of e.employee_no and o.employee_no (a cartesian product of (c,o) and e) to select the records for Lehigh High School.

UNION, INTERSECTION, and DIFFERENCE

The theoretical basis of relational databases is traditional set theory (relational algebra), in which the tables form the sets. The SQL SELECT statement includes the algebraic operators: SELECT (extract **entire** records), PROJECT (extract individual columns from a table or a result table), CARTESIAN PRODUCT (collect data from several tables without a join predicate), and JOIN (collect data from several tables via a join predicate).

Relational algebra also has three other operators, namely INTERSECTION, DIFFERENCE, and UNION. Only the UNION operator appears explicitly in both Oracle and SQL/DS. All three operators work on two or more comparable relations, but in SQL only UNION yields sensible results.

If, for example, we operate on the employee and customer tables, we can issue the following search:

```
SELECT first_name, zip_code
FROM employees
UNION
SELECT company_name, zip_code
FROM customers
```

UNION returns **all the different** records from the two searches as a result table. Both tables may have predicates. For example, consider finding all employees who live in Zip Code 14031 and all customers in the same area. Perhaps we want to invite them to an open house or inform them of a switch in territorial assignments.

```
SELECT last_name, zip_code
FROM employees
WHERE zip_code = '14031'
UNION
SELECT company_name, zip_code
FROM customers
WHERE zip_code = '14031'
ORDER BY 2,1
```

LAST_NAME	ZIP_CODE
Nickels	14031
Lehigh High School	14031
South Ball Club	14031
Klein	14031

To apply the UNION operator, the tables must be comparable. The number and types of elements in the printout lists must be identical (recall that a SELECT statement always forms a new table).

The result table includes all records that satisfy either search. So it includes both employees and customers in Zip Code 14031.

Note that you cannot refer to column **names** in the ORDER BY clause, as they may differ in the two queries. Instead, you must refer to **positions** in the printout list. SELECT statements may generally refer to positions instead of column names. However, you cannot use such references in the printout list itself, because its order determines the numbers (so the references would be circular).

We will not treat INTERSECTION and DIFFERENCE (or MINUS, as it is called in Oracle, which implements both) in depth here. But we will describe them briefly.

INTERSECT returns records that satisfy **both** search criteria. For example, find the names of employees who are in both the employee and the order tables (here INTERSECT must appear in a subquery):

```
SELECT first_name, last_name FROM employees
WHERE employee_no IN
   (SELECT employee_no FROM employees
   INTERSECT
   SELECT employee_no FROM orders)
```

DIFFERENCE (MINUS) returns records that satisfy the first search criterion but **not** the second. The following search returns only employees who do **not** appear in the order table:

```
SELECT employee_no FROM employees
MINUS
SELECT employee_no FROM orders
```

We can do the same searches with the EXISTS or IN operator.

3.3 INSERT

INSERT lets us enter data into a table. We can enter it directly, transfer it via parameters, or select it from another table.

A typical example of entering values directly is:

```
INSERT INTO employees
VALUES(200,'Ivan','Jacobs','67 Elinore Avenue',
   '14300','339-7654','25-JUN-86','T',NULL,1200)
```

This method is practical only for a few records. Even though editors can repeat statements, the command approach leads to a lot of extra typing.

An alternative is to transfer values via parameters. In SQL/DS, a typical command is

```
INPUT employees
```

The table's name appears along with the name, data type, and length of each field. You can then simply type the field values for each record. When you finish, issue an END command.

In Oracle, the command looks like:

```
INSERT INTO employees
VALUES(&1,'&2','&3','&4','&5','&6','&7','&8','&9',&10);
```

If you save the command (as you can in both Oracle and SQL/DS) and execute it with a RUN command, you will be asked to enter the first value, second value, and so on.

The third way to enter data into a table is by transferring it from another table (or several others) by combining INSERT with SELECT. The combination is particularly useful if you want to do the following operations:

- Change the data types in a table, as such a change requires an empty table.

- Store a join of several tables as one table.

- Divide a table into parts.

- Remove a field from a table.

Suppose, for example, you decide that the city field in the zip_codes table is too short. You can lengthen it in two stages. First, create a new table with:

```
CREATE TABLE zip_code_new
(zip_code CHAR(5),
city CHAR(30))
```

Then copy the data to the zip_code_new table with the command:

```
INSERT INTO zip_code_new
SELECT zip_code,city
FROM zip_codes
```

You can, of course, perform SELECT with conditions or subqueries. After copying the data to zip_code_new, you can either delete all the records in the old table and change the definition (Oracle) or completely delete the old table and create a new one (SQL/DS). Finally, you can copy the data back from zip_code_new (and delete it). You must use the same procedure in SQL/DS to change a table's name.

For example, suppose you want to create a table containing the numbers and names of employees along with the orders they handled. That is, you want to join the employee and order tables. Issue the following two commands:

```
CREATE TABLE empl_orders
(employee_no SMALLINT,first_name CHAR(20),
last_name CHAR(25),order_no SMALLINT)


INSERT INTO empl_orders
SELECT e.employee_no,first_name,last_name,o.order_no
FROM employees e,orders o
WHERE e.employee_no=o.employee_no
AND o.shipped IS NOT NULL
```

The empl_orders table gets the employee numbers and names from the employee table, and the order numbers from the order table.

3.4 UPDATE

The UPDATE command lets you change field values. Its general syntax is:

```
UPDATE table_name
SET field_name=new_value[{,field_name=new_value}]…
[WHERE condition]
```

The following example implements a general pay increase of 4% (not even enough to keep up with inflation!):

```
UPDATE employees
SET base_pay = base_pay * 1.04
```

The following example changes string values:

```
UPDATE employees
SET last_name = 'Henderson', type = 'M'
WHERE telephone = '325-5464'
```

Note that you can SET a field to NULL (with field = NULL) even though you must use IS NULL to verify the result.

You can use UPDATE with a subquery. The following command gives all employees who have handled more than four orders a 12% increase in base pay. First, we must search the order table. Then we must update all employee records with numbers in the selected set.

```
UPDATE employees
SET base_pay = base_pay * 1.12
WHERE employee_no IN
    (SELECT employee_no
    FROM orders
    GROUP BY employee_no
    HAVING COUNT(*) > 4)
```

Note that an UPDATE can only operate on one table. The result may be inconsistent. If, for example, a customer orders five handballs (item_no = 4034), we must change three tables. We must add records to the order and order_specs table and update the stock in the inventory table. The procedures are:

```
1   INSERT INTO orders
    VALUES(.....)

2   INSERT INTO order_specs
    VALUES(.....)
```

```
3   UPDATE inventory
    SET quantity = quantity - 5
    WHERE item_no = 4034
```

A similar situation occurs if a customer cancels an order. Again, we must change three tables. Failure to revise any of them will obviously cause problems later. We may have incorrect stock levels, order specifications with no corresponding order, or a nonexistent order.

3.5 DELETE

The DELETE command removes records from a table. It has the following general syntax:

```
DELETE FROM table_name
[WHERE condition]
```

The following command removes employee 77 (who never did anything anyway!):

```
DELETE FROM employees
WHERE employee_no=77
```

A DELETE command with no WHERE condition removes **all** records from the table. The structure remains, but it is empty.

You can use a subquery with DELETE. For example, suppose we want to fire all employees who have handled less than 10 orders. We must make a subquery on the order table, transfer the employee numbers, and use them to delete records from the employee table. Later all we must do is stuff the termination notices in the employees' Christmas cards. "Have a merry Christmas, a joyful New Year, and a good time searching for your next job."

```
DELETE FROM employees
WHERE employee_no IN
    (SELECT employee_no FROM orders
    GROUP BY employee_no
    HAVING COUNT(*) < 10)
```

DELETE can also cause inconsistency in the database. The last command, for example, would leave the order table with entries assigned to people who are no longer in the employee table. Here again, SQL itself has no way of ensuring consistency. Version 2 of SQL/DS solves part of the problem by providing extra clauses for use with the CREATE TABLE command (see Chapter 8). More general solutions are to use SQL statements embedded in a traditional programming language or to issue a series of DELETE commands.

3.6 Views

We have characterized a relational database by suggesting that all data appears to the user to be in tables. The tables are the DBA's primary concern when creating a database. However, users may find that the tables do not contain the appropriate combinations of data for their applications.

To solve this problem, we use another type of table, called a view. The tables we have discussed so far are **base tables**. They have an independent existence, and their data is physically stored somewhere in the system.

Views do not exist physically. They are "virtual tables" that exist only as definitions recorded in the system catalog.

A view is a **way** of looking at base tables or a **subset** of them. Think of it as a window through which users can examine the database. The windows has filters so that only part of the database is visible. Note that searches really occur on base tables, not on views.

Creating Views

The CREATE VIEW command has the following general syntax:

```
CREATE VIEW view_name[[field][{,field}]…]
AS SELECT [DISTINCT] [*|field1[{,field2}]…]
FROM table_name|view_name
[WHERE condition]
[GROUP BY grouping_criteria]
[HAVING predicate]
```

You cannot use an ORDER BY clause in forming a view, since ordering is not part of the underlying table and hence cannot be part of the view either. To delete a view, issue the command

```
DROP VIEW view_name
```

This is like constructing a tall building between your window and the ocean.

We could create the following view (Figure 3-2) for a salesperson whose territory is the Buffalo metropolitan area:

```
CREATE VIEW buffalo_customers
AS SELECT type, customer_no, company_name, telephone
FROM customers
WHERE zip_code > '14031' AND zip_code < '14300'
```

type	customer_no	company_name	telephone

view: buffalo_customers

cust_no	comp_name	street	zip_code	telephone	type

base table: customers

Figure 3-2. Typical view based on the customer table.

From the user's point of view, a table exists with the name "buffalo_customers." We can treat it just like a base table. We can omit the field names from the definition of the view. It then inherits names from the base table. Note one obvious advantage for the user. He or she no longer has to qualify all searches with the extra condition WHERE zip_code > '14031' AND zip_code < '14300'.

Instead, the user can now simply enter:

```
SELECT *
FROM buffalo_customers
```

or include conditions as in:

```
SELECT company_name,telephone
FROM buffalo_customers
WHERE type = 'S'
```

As far as the user is concerned, the other records in the customer table do not exist. It is as if you had put the Buffalo customers' records in a separate table or marked them in a special way.

We refer to the command CREATE VIEW as a declarative statement. All that happens is that we specify the view definition. The SELECT statement to which it is linked is not executed. Instead, the system stores the view name in the catalog along with the SELECT that defines it. So when a user issues the command

```
SELECT * FROM buffalo_customers WHERE type = 'S'
```

the DBMS looks in the system catalog to determine that buffalo_customers refers to a view. It then reads the view's definition and translates the command to a search of the base table, namely:

```
SELECT type,customer_no,company_name,telephone
FROM employees
WHERE type = 'S'
AND zip_code > '14031' AND zip_code < '14300'
```

Views have the following advantages:

- They reduce the number of conditions users must write in common situations.

- They provide security as they conceal data from users who should not see it or have no need to see it.

- They allow the DBA to revise tables without affecting users. All he or she must do is revise the view definitions so the users see the same data as before.

- They allow users to work with virtual columns, i.e., ones derived from other columns.

- They let users change column names and use a different order than in the original base table.

- They are dynamic, that is, they change automatically when changes occur in the database tables upon which they are based.

- They do not use any storage except for their definitions.

So far, our views have inherited field names from the base table. This is not necessary, nor do fields have to appear in the same order as in the base table. For example, consider the following view of employees in department A20. It includes only certain fields and assigns the salary field a new name.

```
CREATE VIEW A20 (last_name,first_name,salary)
AS SELECT last_name,first_name,base_pay
FROM employees WHERE department = 'A20'
```

The advantages of views become more obvious with complex searches. Less typing is perhaps less important than the fact that the view is a proven approach. You do not have to worry about either typing or structural errors. The view automatically includes the conditions specified when creating it.

Manipulating Views

There are restrictions on how we can manipulate views, particularly when using UPDATE, INSERT, or DELETE. Only rarely do problems occur with views involving a single base table. However, no manipulations are allowed if the view definition contains GROUP BY, HAVING, or SELECT DISTINCT.

The reason for eliminating GROUP BY and HAVING is that actual records that can be updated do not exist. With SELECT DISTINCT, the problem is that one record in the view may correspond to several records in the base table. Commands such as UPDATE or DELETE applied to the view may then alter a base table without the user knowing how many records they affect.

All records in a table must be uniquely identifiable, that is, there must be a primary key. The view must contain the primary key from the base table so that one can identify the records to be processed. However, SQL does not support the concept of primary key, so there is no way to insure that this condition holds.

What happens if you create a view without a primary key? And what if you try, for example, to delete a record from it? You should not be able to do so because you cannot be sure of which records or how many are involved. SQL/DS provides a message indicating that the command will affect several records. Oracle simply does what it is told.

INSERT has the added requirement that the view must include all NOT NULL declared columns in the base table. Otherwise, the

DBMS will try to insert a NULL value into a NOT NULL column, producing an error message.

What about commands that remove records from a view? Suppose we create a view for department A20 using:

```
CREATE VIEW A20
AS SELECT * FROM employees
WHERE department = 'A20'
```

We then execute the following command:

```
UPDATE A20
SET department = 'A30'
WHERE employee_no = 33
```

Employee 33's record should immediately disappear from the view. This is an odd breach of security if we created the view to restrict the user to working with data related to department A20. The effect is somewhat like giving an employee the right to reclassify a document to a level that he or she lacks the clearance to read.

The ANSI standard provides the clause WITH CHECK OPTIONS as a qualifier to the CREATE VIEW command. The idea is that the DBMS should check the consequences before updating a view. If the revised record ends up no longer belonging to the view, the change is not allowed. Neither SQL/DS nor Oracle implements WITH CHECK OPTIONS.

Virtual Columns in Views

As mentioned, we can define views to include virtual columns, i.e., ones not actually present in a base table. A virtual column appears as a computed value in a printout. It may be the result of a GROUP BY (which in general cannot be updated), or it may be a derived column computed from visible columns.

For example, the following view shows items that are low in stock (within 20% of the order level):

```
CREATE VIEW reorder
(item_no, item_name, quantity, order_level, difference)
AS SELECT item_no, item_name, quantity, order_level,
    quantity - order_level
FROM inventory
WHERE quantity < order_level * 1.2
```

Note that because the column "difference" is not in the base table, we cannot omit the field names from the view definition. We must specify all of them.

We can now list items that are out of stock or close to it with the following command:

```
SELECT * FROM reorder;
```

ITEM_NO	ITEM_NAME	QTY	ORDER LEVEL	DIFFERENCE
4028	Jersey (basketball)	22	20	2
4029	Basketballs	22	20	2
4085	Shorts (medium)	34	30	4
4093	Tennis racket	20	18	2
4094	Tennis net	17	18	-1

Note the following when working with derived columns:

SELECT: You can select from views with virtual columns, and you can refer to the virtual columns in the condition part of a query. For example, the following is legal:

```
SELECT * FROM reorder
WHERE difference > 2
```

UPDATE: You cannot update virtual columns. After all, what would you change?

INSERT: You can insert new records into a view, but you cannot insert values into virtual columns. You must specify the fields into which values are to be inserted. All NOT NULL fields must be in the view definition. The following is, therefore, legal:

```
INSERT INTO
reorder(item_no,item_name,quantity,order_level)
VALUES(4099,'Shin protectors',100,30)
```

DELETE: You can delete all records from a view
                containing virtual columns. You can also
                delete selected records by referring to the
                virtual columns. The primary key and NOT
                NULL are meaningless.

Views Involving Several Tables

Suppose we want a report on orders over $600, including company
names, item numbers, quantities, prices, and totals. The search involves many tables and many conditions, so a view is useful here. If
we create it correctly, we know we have the right result.

```
CREATE VIEW large_orders AS
SELECT c.company_name, os.order_no, os.item_no,
    os.quantity, i.price, os.quantity * i.price "TOTAL"
FROM order_specs os, inventory i, customers c,
    orders o
WHERE c.customer_no = o.customer_no
AND o.order_no = os.order_no
AND os.item_no = i.item_no
AND os.quantity * i.price > 600
```

We can then execute the following search:

```
SELECT company_name, item_no, quantity, price, total
FROM large_orders;
```

COMPANY_NAME	ITEM_NO	QTY	PRICE	TOTAL
Jack's Exercise Studio	4024	20	43	860
East Side Club	4034	20	32.1	642
Jack's Exercise Studio	4034	20	32.1	642
South Ball Club	4056	20	43.7	874

We can also put conditions on the derived columns, such as:

```
SELECT company_name, total
FROM large_orders
WHERE total > 700
ORDER BY total
```

Furthermore, the SELECT statement that defines the view may contain a GROUP BY or a GROUP BY xxx HAVING yyy.

The restrictions on updating views formed from a table also apply here. However, they do not matter, as another rule takes precedence anyway: **One can never update a join**, that is, one cannot use UPDATE, INSERT, or DELETE. So the only way you can use views formed by joining tables is in SELECT statements. This may seem strange, because all fields are linked to tables, so they should be updated correctly. The problem is maintaining consistency. The user has no way of knowing the origins of the various fields, so there is no way to reflect changes in the join back to the actual fields.

Views on Views

Because a user perceives a view as just another table, he or she may want to create views based on other views. After all, a structured language should allow recursive substitution. For example, the following statement creates the view buffalo_sales based on the view buffalo_customers:

```
CREATE VIEW buffalo_sales (company_name, total_sales)
AS SELECT b.company_name, SUM(price)
FROM buffalo_customers b, orders o, order_specs os,
    inventory i
WHERE b.customer_no = o.customer_no
AND o.order_no = os.order_no
AND os.item_no = i.item_no
GROUP BY company_name
```

Joining a base table with a view is acceptable, as is combining independent views. There are, however, two limitations to consider. One is that a view formed using GROUP BY, DISTINCT, or a built-in function cannot become part of other views.

Also a domino effect may occur if you delete a base table or a view on which another view is based. All derived views will disappear and all programs that use them will fail.

Administration of Base Tables

DBAs often prefer to define a view for each base table that is just an exact copy of it. All manipulations of such views are valid, because the restrictions do not apply to views that are exact copies of an existing table. The strategy can simplify the DBA's work when changing a table structure. Consider, for example, the model shown in Figure 3-3.

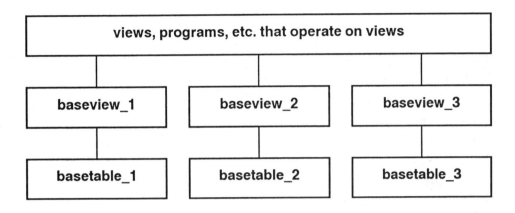

Figure 3-3. Views formed as copies of the base tables.

The strategy is advantageous for the DBA if he or she wants to do any of the following operations:

- Store basetable_3 on various storage media.

- Split a base table or combine tables.

- Save a column in a base table as a different data type or with a different length or precision.

The best approach is to form views of all base tables, then use the views everywhere. Later, if the DBA alters a table, all he or she must do is redefine the base view. The DBA need not alter programs, views, or stored routines that depend on the base view. They will continue to operate as if nothing had happened.

Materializing Views

One problem with views is that they do not refer to physically exist-ing tables. All operations on them are indirect, via the definitions in the system catalog. We could compare the process to selecting partic-ular entries from a card file, based on a written key. Clearly, perfor-mance suffers. Furthermore, if you use the same view often, the system must implement the same indirect process every time with the same results.

What is the solution? Make the view into a base table and copy the data into it. We refer to this as **materializing** the view (sounds al-most supernatural!). Not only is the indirection via the catalog now unnecessary, but the various restrictions on manipulating views no longer apply. The result is higher speed and more flexibility. How-ever, materializing a view also introduces consistency problems, as the view and the original base table are now stored separately. For more information about materializing views, see C. Kung, "Object Subclass Hierarchy in SQL: A Simple Approach," *CACM*, 33:7, July 1990, pp. 117-125.

4

Data Control

Chapter 11 describes how the ANSI/SPARC standard divides the database specification into definition levels. One level is the definition of the database as the user sees it. It is thus the level at which the user works. The language that he or she employs is called a "data language". It can be further divided into a "host language" and a "data sublanguage". The host language is typically a standard general-purpose programming language (such as the one used to write the database program itself). The data sublanguage is intended specifically for database applications. SQL is an example. The data sublanguage can be further divided into a "data definition language" (DDL) and a "data manipulation language" (DML).

Chapter 2 dealt with the data definition language, and Chapter 3 with the data manipulation language. In some cases, we refer to a third part of the data sublanguage, namely a "data control language" (DCL). It is **not**, however, a stand-alone language.

This chapter deals with the DCL. It consists of commands that control user access to the database. Thus DCL is concerned with privacy and security issues, that is, determining who has access to objects (such as tables and programs) and what they can do to them (such as delete, append, or search). The task of DCL is to prevent a user from gaining unauthorized or inappropriate access to data.

DCL commands are seldom the only security measures taken to protect a database. DCL-based control, the security-related part of the DBMS, and the computer operating system work together to safeguard data, each in its own way. The goal is to control users' access to such objects as programming languages, text editors, and statistical tools. The operating system cannot generally deal with table or program-level security, as it knows nothing about the entities involved. Instead, the database program must have its own control system (DBMS) with its own security measures and system catalog.

The operating system must ensure that no one can circumvent the security measures introduced by the DBMS. It may, for example, deny users direct access to the physical files or disks containing the database. It may also deny access to certain terminals. Or it may encode or encrypt data before storing it. The idea here is to avoid an "end run" around the security at one level by moving to another.

4.1 User Types

The DBA must authorize each user who wants to access a database. That is, the DBA must specify who can be linked to the database, and what rights they have to it, its individual tables, and their columns.

There are three user privilege levels or user types: DBA, RESOURCE, and CONNECT. You may compare them to the three estates (or classes) in French history (clergy, nobility, and commoners).

The DBA must establish individual users as specified **types** with ID and passwords that give them certain rights. Certain a priori privileges characterize the three types.

Distributors supply a database program with one DBA already set up. His or her ID and password are provided with the manuals. He or she has **all** rights to the database program and to the as yet nonexistent database.

After installing the database program, the DBA must change the user ID and password, as it is accessible to anyone who reads the manuals. The DBA must therefore create a new DBA with a different ID and password. Think of it as giving himself or herself a new name and new identity, as in popular spy movies. In practice, a common security problem (amazingly!) involves installations that never change the initial settings.

After logging into the program, the DBA can create a new identity using the command

```
GRANT DBA TO new_user_ID IDENTIFIED BY new_password
```

Here GRANT means "assign the status of".

Next the DBA must remove the ID and password found in the manual with

```
REVOKE DBA FROM manual_ID
```

REVOKE means "remove the status of".

Now the DBA can proceed to create other users (this sounds almost biblical). The general syntax for creating a new user (or changing the privileges of an old one) is:

```
GRANT [DBA | RESOURCE | CONNECT]
TO user_ID IDENTIFIED BY password
```

```
GRANT CONNECT TO may_do_a_little IDENTIFIED BY
   new_hire
GRANT DBA TO may_do_everything IDENTIFIED BY
   senior_person
```

Let us now describe the privileges associated with the three user types.

A user with CONNECT privileges is a commoner or low person on the totem pole. He or she has:

- Access to the database.

- The right to manipulate data reserved for the user name PUBLIC by a RESOURCE or by a DBA, that is, publicly accessible data. The particular operations that a CONNECT can perform depend on the rights granted to PUBLIC (e.g., with GRANT SELECT ON table_name TO PUBLIC). The default is to GRANT all manipulation rights to PUBLIC, so administrators must specifically establish a security policy.

Note that when we are dealing with an individual user's access to database objects, GRANT means "give permission to".

A user with CONNECT privileges can also be awarded or denied specified rights, such as:

- Permission to see data that others have created, **if** they allow it.

- Permission to change, delete from, and insert information into the tables of other users, **if** they allow it.

A user with RESOURCE privileges is at an intermediate level (like a member of the bourgeoisie). He or she has:

- All rights that accrue to a CONNECT.

- The right to create tables, indexes, and clusters.

- Permission to extend the rights to create tables, indexes, and clusters to other users, that is, to GRANT.

- Permission to grant (or remove) rights (such as select or update) to his or her own objects (including users with CONNECT rights).

- To perform **auditing** with database objects (such as tables, views, or programs) that he or she owns. Auditing (explained in detail later) means to report how each user employs objects.

A user with DBA privileges is an aristocrat. He or she can do the following:

- Anything that users with RESOURCE and CONNECT privileges can do.

- Grant and remove access privileges to the database, i.e., remove users with CONNECT, RESOURCE, and DBA privileges.

- Perform all DML, DDL, and DCL commands on all tables.

- Establish and change the parameters of the database program.

- Establish and change the database's logical and physical structure.

- Backup the database and regenerate damaged databases.

- Audit how users have employed their rights and generally oversee database operations.

- See everything in the system catalog and make limited changes to it.

The DBA is thus the highest authority. A user who has been granted DBA privileges has all rights (including the ability to remove everyone except himself or herself) and correspondingly many obligations. The only thing a DBA **cannot** do is remove the last DBA. Such an action would make the database totally secure and completely inaccessible.

To manage access control, the DBA should change the individual users' passwords occasionally (and remember to tell them about it) with the command:

```
GRANT CONNECT TO may_only_do_a_little
IDENTIFIED BY errand_person
```

Similarly the DBA may remove privileges with

```
REVOKE RESOURCE FROM may_do_a_little_more
```

Or completely deny a user access to the database with

```
REVOKE CONNECT FROM may_do_just_a_little
```

4.2 Controlling Access to Database Objects

Here by "objects", we mean tables, views, and programs, and by "users" we mean individuals or programs that operate on the objects.

The purpose of controlling access to database objects is to enhance privacy and security. This means safety from unauthorized or incorrect use. As a side effect, it also increases the likelihood of keeping the data in the database consistent.

Consistency is mostly a matter of planning, not a privacy or security issue by itself. But the matters are related in that users who know what they are doing and usually do things right also will treat the database better than others. Chapter 8 discusses consistency in detail.

Most organizations have several groups of users. Each of them should have certain privileges (and responsibilities) with respect to tables, columns, and fields. The problems are not simply ones of withholding information or control from certain user categories. Of course, we do not want unauthorized people examining salary information or (even worse) changing it. But we must also prevent users from changing data accidentally, as when someone in the accounting department accidentally overwrites stock levels or prices while computing inventory values.

An important aspect of working with database design and the specification of user access to objects is the establishment of an access matrix (Figure 4-1). It records who has which rights to manipulate the database. It represents the current security state of the system.

object/ user	TAB1	C1	C2	C3	W1	C2
U2	d/i	s	s/u			s/u
U3	s/i/u					
U5				s/u	s	u
PR3	s/d/i					
PR8		u		u		

Figure 4-1. Access matrix.

The primary purpose of the access matrix is administrative, as it documents access rights. The commands GRANT and REVOKE are the practical applications of security measures.

The matrix in Figure 4-1 describes two database objects: table TAB1 (and its columns C1, C2, and C3), and view W1 (with column C2). It also describes users (U2, U3, and U5) and programs (PR3 and PR8). Note that "s" stands for SELECT, "u" for UPDATE, "i" for INSERT, and "d" for DELETE.

For example, user U5 has no general rights to TAB1 but has SE-LECT and UPDATE rights to column C3. User U2 has the right to perform DELETE and INSERT on TAB1 generally, but may only execute a SELECT on C1 and SELECT or UPDATE on C2.

As with access privileges, the commands GRANT and REVOKE delegate and remove rights to individual database objects. GRANT has a single parameter associated with it, namely WITH GRANT OPTIONS.

For example, consider the company accounting department. Its personnel will typically have CONNECT privileges only, for they seldom need to create new tables. They are end users, not programmers or analysts.

Suppose also that the accounting department prints salary schedules and enters or changes salary agreements. An appropriate division of responsibility would be to give one person the right to see and change an employee's salary, whereas another (or another group of users) can only access or print it.

Each group of employees in the accounting department would have its own user_ID. For example, the person who can alter salaries might have user_ID "chief", whereas others have user_ID "disbursers". The DBA must issue two GRANT commands to establish the rights.

As the employee table is accessible by PUBLIC, the DBA must issue a REVOKE ALL FROM PUBLIC command to control what each employee can do. CONNECT users then have no rights to do anything at all. Except perhaps make coffee and run errands.

Now the DBA can link the two types of users (the chief and the disbursers) to the database:

```
GRANT CONNECT TO chief
    IDENTIFIED BY the_boss
```

```
GRANT CONNECT TO disbursers
    IDENTIFIED BY the_secretaries
```

The command **GRANT CONNECT** does not, however, actually give "chief" and "disbursers" any rights (because of the **REVOKE ALL FROM PUBLIC**). So two more commands are necessary:

```
GRANT SELECT, UPDATE ON employees TO chief
GRANT SELECT ON employees TO disbursers
```

You might say that the first two commands give the users a rank or title. The next two give them the authority or resources to match it.

The individual who issues the **GRANT** command is "the grantor", the person who is the object is "the grantee". The terminology apparently comes from either a feudal society or a government bureaucracy.

Both grantees ("chief" and "disbursers") can now perform a SELECT on the employee table. Chief can also perform UPDATEs on the table.

The DBA or a RESOURCE (who created the employee table) should realize that "chief" may be on vacation, ill, out of town, playing golf, or amorously chasing his or her secretary around a desk. To avoid delays and other problems, the administrator adds the proviso **WITH GRANT OPTIONS** to the original **GRANT**. It allows the grantee to extend the same rights to others.

```
GRANT SELECT, UPDATE ON employees
TO chief WITH GRANT OPTIONS
```

The guiding principle is that users who have the right to do something with a database object also can pass on their rights to others. Thus WITH GRANT OPTIONS means that the user is both grantee and grantor of rights to his or her own tables.

Therefore, user "chief" can issue the command:

```
GRANT SELECT, UPDATE ON employees
TO trustworthy
```

From now on, the employee identified as "trustworthy" (or "chief henchperson") can do the same operations as "chief", that is, UPDATE the **entire** employee table.

The user (chief) could also give "trustworthy" fewer rights by specifying columns that he or she can access:

```
GRANT SELECT, UPDATE (base_pay) ON
employees TO trustworthy
```

Since "chief" has SELECT rights to the employee table, he or she can create a view from it, showing just managers:

```
CREATE VIEW managers AS
SELECT first_name,last_name,base_pay
FROM employees
WHERE TYPE='M'
```

and then issue

```
GRANT SELECT,UPDATE (base_pay) ON managers
TO trustworthy
```

A user can thus be assigned the rights to operate on a table and the ability to pass on the rights to others ("chief" grants to "trustworthy" who grants to "also_trustworthy", etc.). To determine who has granted what to whom, a user can refer to a table in the system directory (the *Burke's Peerage* of the database world).

At some point, however, the local pecking order may become so complicated that the user (or the DBA) decides to issue a "REVOKE privilege FROM user" or "REVOKE ALL FROM user" command. When "chief" returns from vacation and learns what has happened, he or she can issue

```
REVOKE SELECT, UPDATE FROM trustworthy
```

The result is that the scheming "trustworthy" loses all rights to the table (unless he or she has also received them from someone else). Furthermore, anyone to whom "trustworthy" has granted rights will now also lose them. The system works like a feudal hierarchy where the subvassals fall when the vassal is beheaded or deposed. You may also think of the fallout as like what happens to the office staff or appointees of a politician defeated for reelection.

Except for CREATE TABLE, the right to perform all commands dealing with data definition and manipulation can be granted to others, along with the ability to extend the rights:

```
GRANT SELECT ON table_name TO user
GRANT DELETE ON table_name TO user
GRANT UPDATE ON table_name TO user
GRANT UPDATE (field_names) ON table_name TO user
GRANT DELETE ON table_name TO user
GRANT INDEX ON table_name TO user
GRANT ALTER ON table_name TO user
GRANT ALL ON table_name TO user
```

The reason why we cannot issue a GRANT CREATE TABLE is that it is built into the "GRANT RESOURCE TO user" command. In SQL/DS, a user with CONNECT privileges can, however, be extended a "private dbspace" in which he or she enjoys all rights.

All GRANT commands can be extended to additional privileges, more tables, or more users, as in:

```
GRANT DELETE, SELECT ON table1, table2, table3
TO user1, user2
```

Administraters should extend rights cautiously. After all, didn't Duncan make Macbeth Thane of Cawdor just as the witches predicted? Newly rewarded users may have even larger prizes in mind.

Or GRANTs can be issued to PUBLIC, so everyone can enjoy the rights, as in

```
GRANT INSERT ON customers TO PUBLIC
```

Now even commoners share the bounty.

Except for GRANT ALL, GRANT INDEX, and GRANT ALTER, all GRANTs can also be issued on views, if their definitions permit it. It is impossible, for example, to issue a "GRANT UPDATE ON view_1 TO user" if view_1 is a join of several tables. Remember that you cannot update a join.

It is indeed possible, however, to grant SELECT on a view without also granting SELECT on tables included in its definition (i.e., the grantee does not get rights to SELECT on the base tables). This is in accordance with the idea of the view as a security measure.

WITH GRANT OPTIONS can be appended to any command. All rights that have been extended can be denied by using the REVOKE command:

```
REVOKE privileges FROM user1,user2
REVOKE ALL FROM PUBLIC
```

Unfortunately, revoking rights is more difficult and less common in practice than granting them.

Access to the database and its objects follows so-called "implicit" rules. That is, once the operating system accepts the user identification and password, the rest of the security task is the job of the database system itself.

Security considerations also affect work involving programs. For example, one can issue an individual GRANT or REVOKE in a way that has nothing directly to do with DML or DDL. The following commands are examples:

```
GRANT RUN ON program_name WITH GRANT OPTIONS
REVOKE RUN ON program_name
```

GRANT RUN applies to programs (written in a high-level language) that issue SQL commands. It means, therefore, that the user can run the executable program "program_name". Within it, however, we can have further security through the explicit use of passwords. The program can simply ask "What is your password?". To proceed, the user must authenticate his or her identity. This form of access control is unrelated to the database's system directory or to the GRANT commands, but it can enhance the security of database objects.

5

Indexes and Clusters

As mentioned previously, the definition of the relational database does not specify the physical location of data in mass storage or how it is accessed. Nevertheless, this chapter deals with indexes (and clustering) as they relate to SQL. The basic reason is that indexes are essential to effective use of a relational database. They lead to higher search speeds and accessible primary keys as unique identifiers for records.

This chapter consists of three sections. The first two treat indexes, first in general and then as they apply to relational databases. We will deal specifically with B^+-trees. The last section describes clusters, a way of controlling the physical placement of data in mass storage.

5.1 Purpose and Implementations of Indexes

In an unindexed table, the search for a particular record is sequential, as the table data is stored sequentially on disk. The computer copies individual records (or groups of records) from disk to memory (RAM), where it examines them.

For example, to locate all orders handled by employee 12, the computer must move all records in the order table from disk to RAM. Each time a block of data is transferred, the disk system must move the read/write head before it can transfer the next block (ignoring the fact that some records are already in system buffers). If the table is large, the process involves many input/output (I/O) operations, as the DBMS must move the data a block at a time.

Indexing a table has the sole purpose of **reducing** the number of I/O operations. Thus one can say that indexing is not **necessary** to work with relational databases, as the system could fetch all records sequentially. However, the process will be slower than with indexed tables, much slower in practical situations involving thousands or even millions of records.

To use a book as an analogy, an index does not affect its design, contents, or organization. But it does make the retrieval of information faster and more convenient. Similarly, indexing a table has no effect on its physical characteristics or storage method. The table is still stored sequentially, but the DBMS can use its associated index to search for particular records. One can, therefore, discuss an "indexed sequential file". Note that we emphasize **searching** for data, as it is an essential part of other operations such as updating or deleting. You must find records before you can do anything to them.

An index is an "access strategy", that is, a way to search for records. Indexes are essential only to increase the speed with which the DBMS can locate records.

Databases are often part of on-line systems where response times are critical. For example, consider a bank that must find a particular customer's account among 100,000 for check or credit verification. The customer becomes quite annoyed at a delay of more than 30 seconds. Or consider an airline reservation system that must determine immediately whether there is room on a flight to Beirut (assuming anyone wants to go there these days). Indexing is essential if the user is to obtain an answer quickly. Surely the prospective traveler would not want to wait on the telephone for more than a minute.

In batch jobs (such as printing payroll checks or invoices), indexes are not as important. One reason is that such jobs typically process an entire file anyway. Everyone must get a paycheck or a bill. Another reason is that organizations often run these jobs at off-peak times or in background mode, so direct, rapid access to the data is unnecessary. Indexing is valuable only in applications that must find individual records quickly.

An index is based on a table's data fields. Indexing involves forming a new table with just two fields: a data field that contains the index value and an address field that indicates where the individual records are in mass storage. Note the similarity to the index in a book.

For example, suppose we form an index on the field employee_no in the employee table. The employee table does not change at all, but a new index table is created (see Figure 5-1).

employee_no	RID
1	0.11.12
2	0.11.13
.	.
.	.
12	0.11.14
13	0.11.14

Figure 5-1. Table formed by indexing the employee table on employee_no.

Not only is the index table much smaller than the data table, but its values also form an **ordered list**. The address field identifies the original record via a Record Identification (RID). The RID points to the original record, or more precisely, to the disk block containing it.

The RID's here are arbitrary. In practice, they indicate the number of the specific block in a particular physical file. When the address specifies just the block number, we say it forms a "non-dense index". In other cases, the pointer indicates exactly where the specific data is stored. We then say it forms a "dense index".

The index is stored with the table. Instead of searching the table sequentially, an inquiry for a particular employee starts with a lookup operation on the index. This means many fewer I/O operations, as the index itself (or most of it) can be RAM-resident.

The DBMS searches the index sequentially until it finds the first entry with the desired employee_no. Then all it must do is read the pointer and fetch the record to which it refers. Afterward, the search continues with the next index entry. The system fetches the record, reads the next index value, and so on. The search ends as soon as the system reads an index value that differs from the desired one.

Say, for example, we want to find employee 12. The system reads the index into RAM, and searches it sequentially until it finds value 12. It reads the address, and fetches the block containing the record. The search through the index continues. However, as the next entry is 13 and the index is ordered, the search ends. In contrast, a sequential search would have to examine the entire table to be sure there were no more entries with the desired employee_no.

Let us now assume that the order table has 50,000 records. Creating an index on order_no causes the access time (the time it takes to find the desired record) to vary for different records. The reason is that the DBMS cannot store the entire index in RAM, so it must do I/O operations to fetch parts of the index as needed. Each time it loads a new part into RAM, it must search it sequentially. The variable access time is annoying to database users, as it introduces unpredictability into standard operations. Not knowing exactly how long a job will take can have a major effect on one's schedule.

5.2 Creating and Using Indexes

The solution to the problem for very large indexes is to form an index to the index. This is, in fact, what happens when one issues a command to create an index. The index is constructed as a so-called "B$^+$-tree". The standardized syntax for creating such an index on a single field is:

```
CREATE [UNIQUE] INDEX index_name
ON table_name
(field_name [ASC | DESC] [,field_name[ASC | DESC]...])
```

The B$^+$-tree, like other indexes, does not alter the storage structure. The only thing that changes is the search strategy. The idea behind the B$^+$-tree is the same one a sensible person would use to guess a number between 1 and 30, assuming the questioner tells you whether your guess is high, low, or on the mark. The sequential method corresponds to guessing each number in order, starting at 1. Obviously, this is very slow and time-consuming unless the number happens to be small. In the B$^+$-tree approach, you always guess the middle of the interval, thus halving the possible range each time. At some point, the interval becomes so small that you can use the sequential technique to find the exact value. This approach, on the average, requires fewer guesses and hence fewer I/O operations than the sequential approach. A rule of thumb is that the number of guesses is roughly the base-2 logarithm of the number of records. A sequential query posed on 50,000 records will, on the average, require examining half the records (25,000!). The B$^+$-tree method, on the other hand, requires examining just 16 entries. Our analysis assumes binary searches (dividing the interval in half each time). Dividing it into thirds or smaller fractions reduces the number of iterations even more.

To index the customer table by customer_no, issue the following command:

```
CREATE UNIQUE INDEX customer_no
ON customer (customer_no)
```

Figure 5-2 shows a model of the B$^+$-tree with customer_no recorded as consecutive numbers. Here we are dividing the intervals into thirds each time.

A B$^+$-tree is a "B-tree" plus a "sequential part". Figure 5-2 shows a B-tree above the dotted line and the sequential part below it. The B-tree itself consists of an array of branches ("nodes"). We can regard the tree as consisting of a division of the indexed data into intervals (depending on both the database system and the indexed data values). At the top of the tree is the first division (the top node, called the **root** despite the biological awkwardness), with the other nodes (the branches) hanging down. No one can accuse computer scientists of knowing much about botany! At each level, there is a new division containing both a data value and the addresses of a new interval.

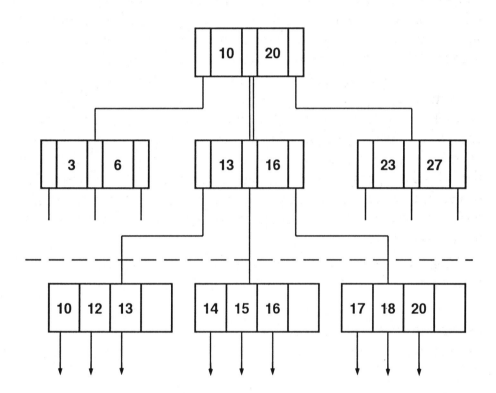

Figure 5-2. Index values organized in a tree structure.

The lowest part is the sequential part, called the "leaves". Each leaf contains, like the preceding nodes, both a data value and a pointer. But instead of pointing to a new node, a leaf pointer points to the record's mass storage address, actually to the block number.

A search for a particular record involves comparing the value with the intervals of the top node. Depending on the result, a pointer directs the search to the next level. A new comparison is made. The process continues until it reaches the last level. There the DBMS does a **sequential** search of the index segment until it finds the correct value. It can use the address of the record directly to locate and fetch the disk block. If the index is unique, there is a pointer for each data value in the sequential part; if it is not unique, there must be at least one pointer.

The number of subdivisions in the nodes is system-dependent, whereas the number of levels depends on the number of index values. In practice, the data values may be distributed unevenly (e.g., 80% of them might be between 1 and 100, and the remaining 20% between 100 and 1000). The number of levels or nodes in the "low end" would then exceed the number in the "high end". The result would be a varied number of searches through the B-tree. In practice, most B^+-trees are "balanced", based on an algorithm that assures that the number of levels through which a search must pass is the same for all records. Just as blocks containing data values will always contain extra room for updates, those containing index values will also have extra room for updating the index. In cases where there is no more room, or if the distribution of data values becomes lopsided, the DBMS must change the individual node intervals. In some cases, it must even replace the top node.

Deleting a record affects the index only in that it renames the pointer from the sequential part. The empty space can then be used for new index values.

If the index is specified as **unique**, the DBMS will not accept two identical values. The entry of a value already present in the index will cause an error message, and the value will not be stored. A unique index is thus just one linked to an input routine that checks whether the value is already present. The routine is also used during updates to avoid changes that produce duplications. It, along with the declaration of the relevant fields, makes it possible to create and maintain a primary key for a table.

Indexes need not, however, be individual columns. An index can also be a combination of fields (a "concatenated index", involving at most 16 columns or 240 characters), such as:

```
CREATE INDEX kmo
ON order(customer_no,employee_no,order_no)
```

All the fields involved must be in the table being indexed. We cannot create indexes based on values from different tables.

The result of indexing on several fields from the same table (as in the last example) is that the first one is ordered in ascending or descending order. The second one is ordered within the values of the first one, and so on.

When using composite indexes in searches, note that for cases involving only the first field, the index will be used as though only that field were indexed. If the search involves only the first and second fields, then only that part of the index will be used, and so on. If the search does not involve the first field, the index cannot be used, as the primary entry point for the ordered list of values is not present. If searches often use the other fields, you should create additional indexes on them to minimize I/O operations. Note that a table can have up to 255 indexes.

Indexes, of course, have both advantages and disadvantages. We emphasize again that they are not essential to performing searches, and they do not affect non-indexed fields.

The advantages are that searches on indexed fields or combinations generally reduce the number of I/O operations. That is, they require fewer I/O operations than sequential searches. The results in some cases may be spectacular. If the index is in RAM, a query involving only its values may not require any disk accesses at all.

A disadvantage is that indexes occupy storage space, although they are generally much smaller than typical tables. After all, indexes have just two fields.

A more serious disadvantage is the need to update indexes when updating tables. This applies not only to updates involving the indexed field itself, but also to ones that change the physical placement of individual records in mass storage. Fortunately, the latter are rare, as there is always room for updating in the blocks holding the records (see the parameter PCTFREE concerning "space definition"). You should, however, note that the entry of new records into a table does not cause constant updating of the index. The system normally uses an "overflow pointer" that points to blocks holding "new additions", whose data values have not yet been entered into the (primary) index. The system updates the index later as part of a general update of the database's organization.

As mentioned previously, a single table can have up to 255 indexes. The time required to update the indexes of small tables is minimal, far less than the savings from indexed searches.

With large tables, however, you must remember that updating indexes can take time. How many you should have depends on how you use the table. A table that never (or rarely) changes can advantageously be made "completely inverted", that is, have an index associated with each field (and every combination of fields). For tables that are constantly changing (e.g., during their creation), the best policy is to have just a few indexes. For tables that are being formed (or changed in a major way), you may want to create indexes **after** making the additions or changes. In this way, you avoid having to update the indexes constantly or move data (index values) to overflow blocks that soon must be changed again anyway.

Just as the user should not have to worry about updating indexes, he or she should not have to worry about where, when, and how searches use them. The DBMS should handle the details. By examining the system catalog, it must determine which tables and columns it will use in a particular search and whether any columns are indexed. Based on this information, the DBMS should optimize the search by determining whether it would be faster to use the indexed columns or do a sequential search.

To remove an index, use the command

```
DROP INDEX index_name
```

It deletes the index but does not affect the table.

5.3 Clusters

The way in which individual tables of a database are physically stored on disk significantly affects the retrieval speed for elements. Which storage technique yields the best response time is not a question directly related to SQL. Nor does it have anything directly to do with the relational data model. One can determine the best storage forms only from knowledge of the hardware and software with which one is working. There is, however, a limit on how many options are available. We should note that storage strategy is not only a question of **how** one stores data, but also of **what** (i.e., what storage medium) and **where**. The options available depend on the hardware and software used. For example, there are more options when using the UNIX or MVS operating systems with direct access to disks than there are on VM systems that do everything indirectly.

In SQL/DS and Oracle, **clustering** is the only way to control the placement of data. In Oracle, clustering is part of SQL*Plus, whereas in SQL/DS, it is an external DBSU (Data Base Services Utility) job.

Because clustering, unlike indexing, involves changing the physical placement of data, tables that are part of clusters can only be arranged in one way. They can, however, still be indexed in many ways.

The word cluster means a grouping or collection. One should cluster records that are logically associated and are often used together. Clustering means that logically associated records (such as orders from the same customer) are stored close together physically. Clustering multiple tables (the maximum is 32) is often called *interfile clustering*. We can also cluster a single table, called *intrafile clustering*. See Chapter 11 for more on clustering.

Intrafile Clustering

Intrafile clustering involves just one table. The result is much like sorting the data according to a field value. Intrafile clustering is the only type allowed in SQL/DS. The system does it by copying data from a table in a certain order to an ordinary file. For example, to cluster the order table, we must select a particular field (the "cluster key"). Suppose we pick customer_no. The system creates the cluster by moving data to a disk file in the order defined by customer_no. Then it fetches the data back in the same order. The result is to store all orders associated with a particular customer close together. To create the cluster, we must also create a non-unique index on the cluster key (a "cluster index").

Interfile Clustering

To cluster multiple tables requires a common field. All instances of it must be the same data type and length and, if the cluster is to work as intended, have the same meaning. The fields need not have the same name. If, for example, you must often generate lists of orders for particular customers, you should cluster the customer and order tables around the field customer_no.

The following commands are Oracle's way of working with clusters. In SQL/DS, as mentioned, you cannot combine tables in the same cluster.

To create a cluster, you must provide the DBMS with information about it. You can do this by issuing a command such as:

```
CREATE CLUSTER sale_employees
(customer_no INTEGER)
```

If you are creating a table, you need not change the CREATE TABLE command itself. All you must do is add an amendment that tells the DBMS to store data in certain locations. Not specific physical locations on the disk, but in a certain (logical) **structure**. **Where the data is stored physically is still irrelevant to both the DBMS and the SQL user.**

To tell the system to store a table in an existing cluster structure, include its name and key in the CREATE TABLE command. An example is:

```
CREATE TABLE sales
(customer_no INTEGER,
employee_no INTEGER,
time_of_sale DATE
price DECIMAL(10,2))
CLUSTER sale_employee(customer_no);
CREATE TABLE customers
(customer_no INTEGER,
name CHAR(20),
street CHAR(20),
```

.

.

```
type CHAR(1))
CLUSTER sale_employee(customer_no);
```

Records inserted into the two tables will be stored consecutively around the value of the cluster column customer_no. Thus records that are logically associated (i.e., have the same customer_no) will be stored in the same data block or, if there is not enough room, in successive blocks. The INSERT command itself need not refer to the cluster structure.

To include a table containing data in a cluster, you must first create a corresponding table with a cluster clause. Then use a command like

```
INSERT INTO orders_new SELECT * FROM orders
```

to move data into the cluster structure.

To insert data into a table, SQL must send a command to the DBMS. And since the DBMS does not work with the physical data but with logical tables and records, it must record the placement of data logically. It does this using so-called "dataspaces" (see Chapter 11). Here we note only that a dataspace is always defined (with a specifically indicated value or a default value) by the parameter PCTFREE=N. PCTFREE indicates how much room in the individual blocks to reserve for updating. Because a cluster places related data in the same blocks, you may want to redefine an old dataspace or create a new one with a PCTFREE value higher than the default. After placing the data in the cluster construction, you can reduce PCTFREE again. The room that has thus been made available can be used for updating records and inserting new ones into the cluster.

A cluster index (Oracle only) is automatically created and maintained on the cluster key. Besides searches, the index is also used when inserting new records.

The user is unaware of clustering. The creation of a cluster does not change the way in which the DBMS handles the data structure. For the DBMS (and the users), the database consists of tables and nothing else. The user need not refer to clusters when doing searches, deletions, updates, or insertions.

The main advantage of clustering tables is fewer I/O operations. The first record is located via the cluster index. The system can then simply read data sequentially until the value of the cluster index changes.

Another advantage is that clustering reduces the amount of stored data, as the values of the cluster columns need only be stored once. For example, if a customer has 50 orders registered, customer_no appears 50 times in a non-clustered structure. Clustering thus reduces the amount of redundant information.

But clustering has disadvantages. First, the PCTFREE parameter causes large segments of each block to remain unused, waiting to be filled. Second, other searches and updates may operate slower, because the cluster groups data in an order that is inappropriate for them. Third, the existence of a cluster means that new records that cannot be placed in the block where they really belong must be placed elsewhere on the disk and be linked via pointers. This fragmentation of table data reduces search speed, so tables that are constantly changing must often be reorganized.

In Oracle, you can remove tables from a cluster by creating a copy (with another name) and moving data from the clustered table to the copy. Next, you remove the original with the command "DROP TABLE table_name". You must then reorganize the "disturbed" cluster.

Information about what clusters exist, which tables form them, and which columns are involved is in the system catalog tables.

6

System Catalog

The basic information that the DBMS uses to manage the database is in the "system catalog" or "data dictionary". It is the database's central records of its own contents. As indicated in Chapter 1, the theory of relational databases insists on a clear separation of logical and physical levels. The concepts of physical and logical data independence describe this separation. They require that there be no fixed pointers between the logical database, viewed as a set of tables, and the physical database, regarded as bits and bytes. A consequence of this separation is the need for a mapping between individual objects at the physical and logical levels. (Chapter 11 treats the subject in detail). From the user's point of view, the separation means that he or she can regard the database as just a collection of tables.

The system catalog lets the DBMS operate on the logical database. It is the key to deciding how to conduct and optimize searches. The DBMS uses it to decide such issues as whether referenced tables and columns exist, whether any columns are indexed, whether the search can be optimized by using indexed columns, and whether the user has the right to perform the search.

Just like everything else in the database, the system catalog consists of tables (typically between 20 and 40 of them, depending on the software). In contrast to users' data tables, the system itself creates and maintains the catalog. No user (not even the DBA) can create or delete catalog tables, and the DBA can only alter them to a very limited extent. There are thus no CREATE, UPDATE, DELETE, or INSERT commands for the system catalog. On the other hand, commands such as CREATE TABLE or CREATE UNIQUE INDEX not only create objects but also insert information into tables in the system catalog.

The number of tables in the catalog and their structure is product-dependent. They also depend on the type of DBMS in use: single-user or multiuser, PC or mainframe. But although the details vary, the information in the catalog is almost always the same.

Most catalog tables are accessible to everyone. Users can extract data from them with ordinary SELECT commands. They can create views of the tables and join them. By examining the catalog tables, users can determine which indexes, tables, and views they have created. They can also determine the GRANTs they have issued. Typically, the DBA uses the system catalog the most, as he or she must check the daily operation of the database. Some tables are reserved for the DBA's use.

We can divide system catalog tables into three groups that record the **operation, tables,** and **structure** of the database.

6.1 Database Operation

The tables in the first group contain information about what **happens** in the database as it operates. They record which users have access to it and what rights they have.

Tables that record the database's daily operations are primarily intended for the DBA. They are called *audit tables*. The DBA can use them to track how individual users employ the database. The following describes how Oracle records daily operating status. The reason for choosing Oracle is that it treats audit tables like other database tables. SQL/DS, on the other hand, places the audit tables and their contents outside the system catalog. It writes the records of what occurs (the database's history) in an ordinary file.

The audit tables record a great deal of information and are updated constantly during normal operations. In practice, the system reads and writes more information than anyone ever uses. You should thus employ auditing cautiously, as it slows down all productive work. Auditing is, therefore, not automatic. A DBA (or a RESOURCE) must request that it be turned on, and must specify the amount of detail required.

For example, if auditing is active, the following command records all **unsuccessful** attempts to delete, select, alter, or update records in the customer table.

```
AUDIT DELETE, SELECT, ALTER, UPDATE
ON customers BY ACCESS WHENEVER NOT SUCCESSFUL
```

Here the audit tables are also a security measure, since the DBA can record all attempts by an individual to do unauthorized operations. Obviously, no one can enforce a security policy without recording activities.

Figure 6-1 is a typical printout from an audit table, obtained with the following SQL command:

```
SELECT TIME, USERID, ACTION, OBJECT
FROM AUDIT
```

TIME	USERID	ACTION	OBJECT
02:53 pm	KLEIN	SELECT	PUBLIC.CUSTOMERS
01:08 pm	KLEIN	SELECT	PUBLIC.SALES
09:01 am	KLEIN	INSERT	PUBLIC.CUSTOMERS
10:05 am	KLEIN	UPDATE	PUBLIC.CUSTOMERS
03:50 am	JACOBS	DELETE	CHIEF.GRATUITIES
03:59 am	JACOBS	UPDATE	ECO.PAYTABLES

Figure 6-1. Printout of the audit table AUDIT.

This printout assumes the previous AUDIT command that records all unsuccessful attempts to access tables.

The audit could include other information. For example, the DBA could record which columns users operate on or when they log on and from which terminal.

Note that auditing is of no value unless someone examines and analyzes the output. In practice, many audit tables exist only to satisfy regulations and waste space, time, and paper. Figure 6-1, for example, indicates that user KLEIN has tried to do several unauthorized actions. They occurred during working hours, and involved public files containing widely used information. Perhaps the DBA should speak with KLEIN about what she was trying to do. She may need a few additional rights to do her job properly.

JACOBS' infraction seems more serious. It occurred after working hours (what was JACOBS doing on the system at 4 am?)

and involved sensitive tables he has no business examining. KLEIN's errors are understandable, but perhaps a security administrator should talk to JACOBS (in a closed room with his attorney present). Could JACOBS be a famous international spy on a minor rehabilitation assignment? Perhaps he is working for a regulatory agency, a newspaper, or tax investigators. Or maybe he is just an insomniac who counts security violation messages rather than sheep.

The DBA can use audit tables constructively to track the daily operations of the database. He or she may find that some tables get more use than others, or perhaps are used differently than expected. Such anomalies could indicate a need to reorganize the database.

Besides information about table use, the catalog also records who is active and what each one's status is (C: connect, D: DBA, R: resource). Figure 6-2 shows a typical user authorization table.

```
SELECT * FROM USERAUTH
```

USERNAME	PASSWORD	TIMESTAMP	C	D	R
TF	IZMIR	12-SEP-88	Y	Y	Y
SYS	PQ3E=9T]	12-JUL-87	Y		
PUBLIC		12-JUL-87			
SYSTEM	LX?:Dd	13-SEP-88	Y		
GILBERT	NATASHA	13-APR-88	Y	Y	Y
MADISON	HAVANA	17-DEC-88	Y		
LARIMER	SOBRANIE	17-DEC-88	Y		

Figure 6-2. Printout of user authorization table.

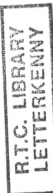

6.2 Database Tables

Another group of system catalog tables contains information about the database tables. This includes users' rights to other users' tables. We will describe some typical examples.

All users can access this group of tables. However, only a DBA can get an overview of everything. Users without DBA status can usually only get an overview of their own area. The DBA can REVOKE and GRANT rights to system catalog tables with commands such as:

```
REVOKE ALL ON SYSTAB FROM KLEIN
```

```
GRANT SELECT ON SYSTAB
TO Klein WHERE CREATOR ='Klein'.
```

Figure 6-3 shows a typical table segment containing information about which names are in use and what types they are.

```
SELECT TNAME, TABTYPE FROM TAB
```

TNAME	TABTYPE
INVOICE	VIEW
HIGH_PRICED	VIEW
FANCY_ORDERS	VIEW
CUSTOMERS	TABLE
ORDERS	TABLE
ZIP_CODES	TABLE
O	SYNONYM
M	SYNONYM
L	SYNONYM

Figure 6-3. Printout from the system catalog table overview.

To see what the customer table looks like, you examine the sys-columns table (Figure 6-4).

```
SELECT CNAME,COLTYPE,WIDTH,NULLS
FROM SYSCOLUMNS
WHERE TNAME = 'CUSTOMERS'
```

CNAME	COLTYPE	WIDTH	NULLS
CUSTOMER_NO	NUMBER	0	NOT NULL
COMPANY_NAME	CHAR	30	NULL
STREET	CHAR	20	NULL
ZIP_CODE	CHAR	5	NULL
TELEPHONE	CHAR	10	NULL
TYPE	CHAR	1	NULL

Figure 6-4. Printout from the system catalog column overview.

You can also get information about views (Figure 6-5) and indexes (Figure 6-6).

```
SELECT VIEWNAME,VIEWTEXT
FROM VIEWS
WHERE VIEWNAME = 'FANCY_ORDERS'
```

```
VIEWNAME          VIEWTEXT


FANCY_ORDERS      SELECT ORDER_NO, OS.ITEM_NO, ITEM_NAME,
                  OS.NUMBER, L.PRICE,
                  OS.NUMBER*L.PRICE
                  FROM OS,L WHERE OS.NUMBER *
                  L.PRICE > 6000 AND OS.ITEM_NO =
                  L.ITEM_NO
```

Figure 6-5. Printout from the system catalog view summary.

```
SELECT TNAME,INAME,COLNAMES,INDEXTYPE FROM SYSINDEXES
WHERE TNAME = 'ORDER_SPECS'
```

TNAME	INAME	COLNAMES	INDEXTYPE
ORDERSPEC	OIND	ORDER_NO	UNIQUE
ORDERSPEC	OIND	ITEM_NO	UNIQUE

Figure 6-6. Printout from the system catalog index summary.

Two index entries with the same name mean that the actual index is a combination of the two fields.

6.3 Database Organization

The third type of system catalog table contains information about the database's physical and logical organization. The information may include lists of:

- Tables and where they are stored physically.

- Spaces (dataspaces) that specify the translation between physical and logical databases.

Figure 6-7 shows a typical listing of information about where individual tables are stored, derived from the command:

```
SELECT CREATOR,NAME,TYPE,STORAGE,EXTENTS
FROM SYSSTORAGE
```

CREATOR	NAME	TYPE	STORAGE	EXTENTS
URSULA	CUSTOMERS	TABLE	10	2
URSULA	INVENTORY	TABLE	10	2

Figure 6-7. Catalog description of where individual tables are stored.

System related tables are typically of no interest to anyone except the DBA. Only a mindless bureaucrat could love such details. He or she can use them to check whether disk space is being used efficiently or whether additional space may be needed soon.

This group of tables also includes ones that describe system programs and other aspects of database operations. For example, tables record the number of locks and deadlocks, commits and rollbacks, physical I/O operations, buffer reads, and log updates. Much of this information is not actually in the system catalog, but is rather kept in independent "utility applications". One reason for the separation is to avoid having so many audits and statistics constantly being updated and written into the catalog. Instead, most typically are in a RAM-resident program, thereby avoiding the need for disk I/O. The contents can, of course, be written to disk for permanent records.

7

Normalization

We have not discussed how many tables our example system requires or how they should be organized. This chapter covers such matters, briefly treating how to achieve the optimum structure for the database. Note that we are referring to the database's **logical** structure and that our optimization involves **logical database** design. We do not consider the physical structure (that is, the storage and access strategies) or physical database design. We also do not consider privacy, security, or integrity issues here. Normalization does not involve any of them.

7.1 Purpose of Normalization

When something must be normalized, presumably it is in an abnormal state requiring correction. For databases, normalization involves making them reflect practical requirements. One might refer to the process as putting the information into an "operational" form. The problem here is selecting what is useful in actual applications. A prerequisite for normalizing a database is that the analyst must know what it represents and how it will be used.

Note that neither the DBMS nor the normalization techniques depend on what the data means. Normalization does not enhance the data's inherent value or significance. It does increase its usefulness and maintainability. There is no special meaning to character combinations such as 1800 or Smith. They become meaningful only in relationships expressed, for example, as earnings(Smith,1800). The **fact** that Smith earns 1800 a month is, however, irrelevant to normalization (despite its importance to the financially hard-pressed Smith family). The reason for its irrelevance is that its meaning is time-dependent. After all, 1800 a month (in unspecified units) was surely once enough to live like a king (well, at least like a duke or baron). Today (or in the near future) it will not be enough to reach the poverty level. The primary goals of normalization are to focus on **time-independent properties** of the underlying relationships such as "earnings(employees,base_pay)".

Before starting normalization, you must decide which objects to use and which properties to operationalize. This job is the DBA's responsibility. If there is only one DBA, the task is not difficult. If there are many, the issues are more complex. The following discussion assumes that the task is solvable — and has been done.

We discuss optimizations in the plural when describing normalization, because there are often several possible design strategies. Some are better than others, but none is **the** only solution. In some cases, a design may be appropriate for a while, but other solutions may become preferable as actual needs change (new objects appear, the company expands, new reporting requirements or applications occur, etc.).

Rather than thinking of normalization as a fixed procedure, you should regard it as a process for achieving the most practical structure for the data. The questions are which data is essential and what relationships exist among its components. When we refer to data subsequently, we mean operational data.

One purpose of normalization is to find and isolate time-independent properties. Such isolation can save storage space. For example, each address commonly includes city, state, and Zip Code. But there is a time-independent relationship between Zip Code and city and state. So we could just keep Zip Code in the address records and use a separate table to determine city and state.

Another purpose is to remove **redundant** information. This can, for example, be multiple copies of data about an individual (such as name, address, or telephone number) stored in several tables. Redundant information is thus extra copies stored in several places in the database.

Obviously, one would prefer to eliminate redundancy from the logical design to reduce storage requirements and simplify maintenance. At the same time, paradoxically, an optimum design may require its reintroduction. The reintroduced information may provide a straightforward way to organize and query the database. Redundancy often saves I/O operations and increases performance.

A third purpose of normalization is to provide unique identifications for individual records. That is, it ensures the existence of a primary key. For example, say the company has two employees named John Smith. It is impossible to uniquely determine John Smith's pay from his name alone. The question: "What does John Smith earn?" may return either 1800 or 1600. The response thus depends on chance or time, because there is no primary key that uniquely identifies each employee.

We do not suggest that normalization is an objective process. It is not. Instead, it is a set of rules of thumb or a checklist that is useful but not essential. Applying normalization effectively depends on six basic requirements:

- Common sense.

- Knowledge of the **meaning** of the data with which one is working. For example, one must be aware of the difference between customers and employees. Normalization is thus largely **semantic** analysis.

- Knowledge of which processes, tasks, and data are actually significant to the company that owns the database.

- Allowing the data structure to accommodate real world uses rather than limiting uses to those readily permitted by the data structure.

- The ability to handle changes, new connections, and new needs.

We can divide normalization into six components. Each contributes to meeting the goal of having all time-dependent properties specified in independent tables representing time-independent relationships. Note that we are still dealing with structural elements. In these relationships or tables, all elements (records) must be uniquely identifiable via primary keys. The concept of primary key is not a structural element but a semantic one. That employee_no identifies an employee uniquely is something **we** know - the DBMS does not. However, in SQL/DS Version 2, Release 2, the primary key has become a structural element with the clause PRIMARY KEY(). Normalization often complicates the structure of the database, as it increases the number of tables. The complexity is a tradeoff for simplifying the structures of the individual tables and recording only essential connections. Furthermore, the connections between individual tables become visible, reducing the likelihood of inconsistency.

Here we emphasize first through third normal forms (hereafter abbreviated as 1NF through 3NF). In practice, a database normalized to 3NF will usually be an optimized structure. We only briefly discuss fourth and fifth normal forms.

Normalization (logical database design) belongs in the first phases of system analysis. Before normalizing the data, we should determine what practical applications require. This will affect how far we carry normalization and how much of its results we use, even though it has no effect on the process itself. We can make the determination in two ways, either by simply listing all possible data, or by defining in advance which actual elements data is to represent. We often refer to the elements as **entities**. There is in principle no difference between the two methods. In either case, we must search for hidden time-independent properties. To emphasize normalization as a **process,** we use the first method here.

The following information (Table 7-1) is necessary for the company database. We have omitted some information from our previous tables because it is not essential to discussing normalization. Note that we omitted everything about customers (except customer_no). Thus we are characterizing a company through its employees and the orders they have taken.

Table 7-1. Example of Essential Company Data

BASIC DATA

last_name

zip_code   Basic data about individual employees

city

type   Employee type (dealer, manager, or
                salesperson)

order_no/   Used with the salary schedule to record
customer_no   who sold what to whom

item_no   Unique identification of an individual item

item_name   Not unique

quantity   Number of a particular item_no currently
                on hand

base_pay   Employee's monthly base salary, depends on
                employee type

7.2 Unnormalized Tables

The requirements for a table to be in 1NF is exactly what relational database theory specifies as essential. That is, a table in a relational database must always be in 1NF.

The two requirements to satisfy are: 1) There must be a **primary key**, and 2) All data values must come from sets (domains) consisting of **atomic** values.

Primary Key

The first requirement for a table to be in 1NF is that it **must** have a primary key. A primary key is, as noted earlier, a field or combination of fields that identifies a record uniquely. To avoid confusion with physical fields (which can be Pascal or FORTRAN file elements or relational definitions), Codd calls the table elements "attributes". He also uses the term "relation" for what others call a table. He wants to distinguish between a relational table and ones used in other types of databases, and also between it and a record in a programming language. In fact, the relational table has characteristics that distinguish it from other tables. But because "relation" is used in so many other situations, we will still refer to **tables**. A (relational) table is defined by its attributes. A subset of them is the primary key, the rest are "non-key attributes".

The primary key is an attribute or combination of attributes that satisfies the following requirements:

- Its value is NOT NULL, that is, no attribute that is part of it may be NULL. Remember, we know nothing whatsoever about NULLs.

- Its value is unique. A table must never have two identical values of the primary key. We also describe this situation as **functional independence** between the primary key and the non-key attributes.

- No **subset** of a primary key may be a primary key by itself. We refer to this as the **minimality requirement**.

If we consider the employee data from our original example (see Chapter 1 and Appendix A), we can show that a primary key exists. In fact, we can find many of them. Some examples are:

```
First_name
First_name + last_name
First_name + last_name + telephone
```

Some might not always be able to serve as primary keys. For example, another employee could be hired with the same first name, telephone number, or even first and last names (such as Robert Smith or Jim Jones). If a primary key could cease to qualify later, we must reject it as a practical solution.

Another problem with the combined primary keys we suggested is that the first name by itself can also serve as a primary key. This violates the minimality requirement. In general, candidate primary keys formed by combining fields may provide unique identifications, but often have subsets that can be primary keys by themselves.

General rules for selecting a primary key are:

- Select one that can **always** act as the primary key, not just for the current data.

- Select one that involves as few fields as possible, both to make it easy to work with, and to meet the minimality requirement.

As mentioned, there may be several fields or combinations of fields that can serve as primary keys. We call them *candidate primary keys*. We select one as the primary key, and make all others suffer the humiliation of being degraded to "candidate keys" (like the runners-up in a beauty contest). In practice, we often introduce an extra field that we know can function as a primary key. Here the field is employee_no. Similarly, we can introduce item_no, customer_no, and order_no as primary keys for items, customers, and orders, respectively. Such selected primary keys are usually integers, because they are the fastest to work with, require little storage, and are easy to generate. On the other hand, note that we are introducing redundant information, as the combination of all fields in a table definition is already unique. But the additions turn out to be a good long-term investment.

Atomic Values

The second requirement for a normalized (1NF) table is that all data values must come from domains with only atomic values. Another, no less cryptic, way of expressing this is that the table may not contain any "repeating groups". The following is an explanation.

In reality, employees typically handle many orders (order_no's), and orders contain many items (item_no's). In implemented form, a typical section of unnormalized data looks like:

```
employee_no    33
first_name     John
last_name      Smith
```

.

.

.

```
customer_no    1002  1005  1006  1002  1005  1006
order_no       2001  2002  2007  2001  2002  2007
item_no        4056  4022  4013  4086  4024  4014
```

Customer_no, order_no, and item_no form a non-atomic, repeating group, as values appear more than once. The repetition causes many problems, so many that relational databases do not allow repeating groups at all. If they were permitted, **the placement** of individual data values would be significant. For example, to determine which customer_no employee 33 had served, we would need to know the **positions** of the data values. The same would be true if we wanted to update or insert data in a record. This would violate the rules of physical and logical data independence.

The problem becomes more acute when one considers manipulations. Repeating groups destroy the uniqueness of employee_no, customer_no, order_no, and item_no. So there is no way of claiming that order 2007 belongs to customer 1006, who purchased items 4014, 4012, and 4021, without assigning meaning to the positions.

Relational databases do not allow repeating groups, whereas hierarchical databases, network databases, and inverted lists all do, for they are much more closely associated with the physical organization of data on a disk.

7.3 First Normal Form (1NF)

How can we handle repeating groups in the actual table? We simply put it into 1NF.

As noted earlier, a table is in 1NF if and only if:

- A primary key exists.

- All attributes are atomic.

To record repeating groups sensibly, we must introduce redundant information, as the next example shows.

Such information solves the difficulty with repeating groups for now, but not if we must record more orders per customer and items per order. If one keeps storing all data in a table, it will eventually become enormous and contain a huge amount of redundant information, as shown in the following example:

last_name	base_pay	empl_no	cust_no	order_no	item_no
Smith	18000	33	1002	2001	4014
Smith	18000	33	1002	2001	4012
Smith	18000	33	1003	2001	4021
Smith	18000	33	1005	2009	4001

Note how many times pieces of information repeat, and consider how little data has actually been recorded. The primary key becomes so complex that it is difficult to find individual data elements. The result is to make table manipulations slow and awkward.

Redundant information obviously increases storage requirements. The extra storage means that it takes longer to locate a record because of the need for more disk transfers. It also slows both log and archival routines, because they must record more data.

In the current simplified case (Table 7-1), we must select a combination of employee_no, order_no, and item_no as a primary key to identify orders containing several items. If we also record base data about customers, the primary key should involve customer_no as well. But although this approach can identify individual records, it creates serious problems when doing standard operations. Note the following difficulties.

Insert: We cannot create a record for a new employee **unless** he or she has expedited at least one order. The person is like a man without a country (or even worse, without a place in the employee file) until that first order arrives. The reason is that no component of the primary key may be NULL, so we need an order number and an item number as well as an employee number.

Update: If an employee gets a raise, we must update **many** records in the employee table. The potential for inconsistency is obvious.

Delete: If we delete an employee from the table, and he or she is the only one who has served a particular customer, both the customer and the order disappear as well. The effect is like bidding goodbye to a freeloading relative who happens to have social connections or press passes to every event in town.

The problem is still the repeating groups. To solve it, we must remove them from the base table. We must decompose it via lossless projection to form new tables.

When discussing decomposition, removal, or isolation of groups or attributes here, we describe the process more precisely as **projecting** a table. The word "projection" comes from the theoretical basis of the relational database (relational algebra). It means that a subset of the table's (the relation's) attributes define a new independent table. (Compare it to the SQL SELECT command, which also creates a new, though temporary, table from the base table.)

When used in normalization, a projection does not just print the repeated groups. The attributes projected into independent tables are

removed from the original table. Also one must introduce or repeat information (and thereby add redundancy) in the new table to prevent meaningful information from disappearing.

Decomposition starts with the first repeating group that is projected into a new table. The algebraic foundation provides no way to project into several tables at once, but it can be done in practice.

Note in the next example that the projection must move the employee_no field into both the orders_1 table and the employees_1 table so the decomposition does not destroy any relationships. We thus retain the links between employees and orders. Note that item_no is part of the primary key for orders_1. So one must know the item numbers to uniquely identify which items (item_name and quantity) are part of a particular order.

The first projection produces the following two tables (with primary key components in italics):

Table: employees_1	Table: orders_1
employee_no	*order_no*
last_name	*item_no*
zip_code	employee_no
city	customer_no
type	item_name
base_pay	quantity

We have thus decomposed the original base table.

Both new tables are in 1NF, as each has a primary key. There is a functional dependence between the primary key and non-key attributes, so there is a one-to-one correspondence between the primary key value and the combination of the other non-key attributes. Furthermore, there are no repeating groups.

But there are still problems that make this solution unsatisfactory. The orders_1 table is the source of them. Note the following about operations on it:

Insert: We cannot add a new item to the database until someone orders it, because no component of the primary key (such as order_no) may be NULL. Advance sales are a good idea, but it would be nice to record what we are trying to sell.

Update: If an item (for any reason) has its name changed, we must update **many** records in the orders_1 table. The result may be inconsistency.

Delete: If we delete a record from the orders_1 table, and it is the only one that refers to an item, the information about the item disappears. For example, we no longer know its name. If we ever get another order for it, we will not even know what it is. Just tell the warehouse manager, "Ship a dozen 4027's" and let him or her find them.

7.4 Second Normal Form (2NF)

To be in 2NF, a table must be:

- In 1NF

- Have all non-key attributes be fully functionally dependent on the primary key.

"Fully functionally dependent" means that the non-key attributes must not be uniquely identifiable from a subset of the primary key.

The purpose of converting a table from 1NF to 2NF is first to solve the insertion and deletion problems described for 1NF. Second, we can then isolate time-independent attributes that might otherwise hide among time-dependent attributes and be a source of inconsistency. The presence of time-independent relations among the time-dependent ones is the source of the above mentioned problems in the 1NF table structure.

The employees_1 and orders_1 tables are both in 1NF. As 2NF requires that all non-key attributes must not be uniquely identifiable from a subset of the primary key, employees_1 is also in 2NF because its primary key is a single field. Orders_1 is not in 2NF, as you can see from the functional dependency diagram of its structure (Figure 7-1).

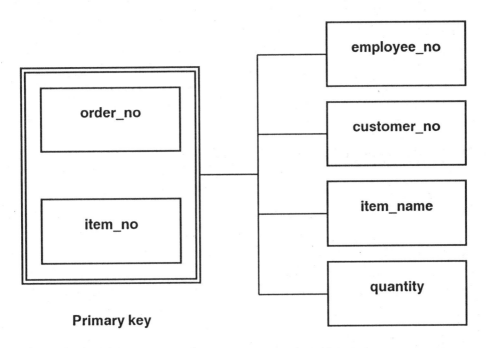

Figure 7-1. Functional dependency diagram for the orders_1 table.

Figure 7-1 shows that a functional dependency exists between the complex primary key and the non-key attributes. If you know the order number and item number, you can determine the item's name and the quantity involved in a particular order uniquely. However, we are not dealing with a "fully" functional dependency because an item's name is uniquely identifiable from its number alone. Similarly, there is a unique dependency between an order number and the employee who handled it. In other words, there exist time-independent relationships between item_ no and item_ name, and between order_no and employee_no. The dependencies, involving only a subset of the primary key, are the reasons why the table is not in 2NF.

To put the orders_1 table in 2NF, we must use projection. We must separate the dependencies by establishing the following two independent tables. The primary key components appear in italics. The order table specifies the customer and employee involved in each order. The order_specs_1 table describes the order's components (items and quantities).

Table: order	Table: order_specs_1
order_no	*order_no*
employee_no	*item_no*
customer_no	quantity
	item_name

However, the solution is still unsatisfactory. The projection does not put order_specs_1 in 2NF, as Figure 7-2 shows. There is a functional dependency between the complex primary key and the non-key attributes. If we know both order_no and item_no, we can determine uniquely the item's name and the quantity involved in an order. But the dependency is not "fully" functional because item_name can be determined from item_no alone. Those two fields have a time-independent relationship.

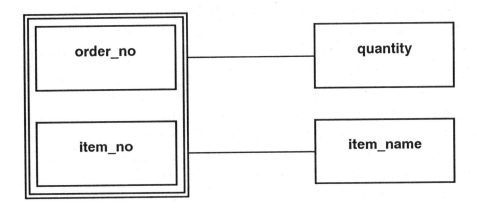

Figure 7-2. Dependencies in the order_specs_1 table.

We can also bring order_specs_1 into 2NF by projection. We project the dependencies that are not fully functional into independent tables. The result is the following two tables.

Table: order_specs	Table: inventory
order_no *item_no* quantity	*item_no* item_name

Everything (order, order_specs, and inventory) is now in 2NF. However, problems still remain. The order part is fine, as the order, order_specs, and inventory tables are now also in 3NF (see the next section), but the employees_1 table is not.

The cause of the problem is hidden time-independent relationships in the table structure. If we assume that a certain type of employee has a certain salary, and that a certain Zip Code refers to a certain city, there are hidden dependencies leading to the following problems.

Insert: We cannot do calculations for a new type of employee (for example, part-time employees) until one has been created (because employee_no must not be NULL). Nor do we have a way to record information about a city in the database until an employee is living there.

Update: If the company increases the base pay of managers, we must update each one's record, introducing many error possibilities. If the relationship between zip_code and city changes, we will also have to update many records. Another kind of error may occur here because other tables use the relationship between zip_code and city. The problem thus could affect the integrity of the database. To keep it accurate and consistent, we will have to update many **tables**, not just many **records**. (More details on this appear in Chapter 8 on integrity.)

Delete: If employees 17, 22, and 31 are laid off (deleted), not only is the information about them removed, but also the fact that an employee of type S (salesperson) has a base pay of $1500. We can happily reduce overhead by firing helpless people right and left, but we cannot afford to lose our salary schedules! Also, if employee 22 is deleted, the city of Olean disappears from our records as well. Cities will thus come and go like the famous Brigadoon, the legendary Scotch village that appears every 100 years or so.

7.5 Third Normal Form (3NF)

1NF is concerned with the primary key and 2NF with the relationship between it and non-key attributes. 3NF deals with the internal relationships among non-key attributes. It says that all of them must be mutually independent.

The requirement for a table to be in 3NF is as follows:

A table is in 3NF if and only if it is in 2NF (and thus also in 1NF) and all non-key attributes are "non-transitively dependent on the primary key". This is the equivalent of saying that a non-key attribute must be solely dependent on (determined by) the primary key, not by anything else.

Figure 7-3 is a functional dependency diagram for the employees_1 table. Note that besides the normal functional dependencies, dependencies exist internally between non-key attributes, that is, between zip_code and city, and between type and base_pay.

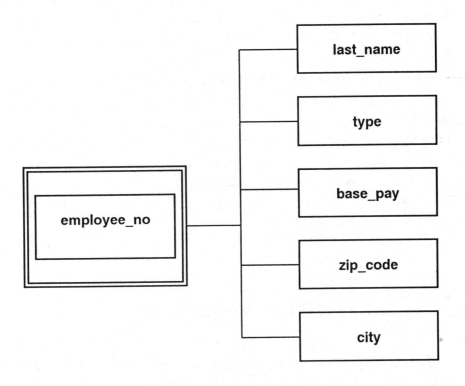

Figure 7-3. Transitive dependencies in the employees_1 table.

The dependency is not like the time-dependent relationship between first_name and zip_code (for example, at a given time, Smith lives in Zip Code 14150). The characteristics are time-independent because a certain type (manager, salesperson, or sales representative) **always** will be tied to only one value of base pay. In the same way, a certain Zip Code is always linked to a city. There is no uniqueness the other way, that is, from base_pay to type, or from city to zip_code. After all, many jobs could have the same base pay and large cities include many Zip Codes.

The technical way to express this is to say that the relationship employee_no —-> district is "transitive" over zip_code, and so is the relationship employee_no —-> base_pay over type. Converting a table from 2NF to 3NF involves isolating all transitive dependencies and projecting each time-independent characteristic into its own table. The result here is the following three tables:

Table: employee	Table: zip_code	Table: type
employee_no last_name zip_code type	*zip_code* city	*type* base_pay

It is questionable whether the last decomposition is useful in practice. Its immediate advantage is that it saves space. Tables containing addresses need only have the Zip Code, not the city as well. For example, if city is a 30-character field and we have 10,000 records, the savings are 3MB of disk space. The other advantage is that Zip Code changes affect only the zip_code table. We could deal with the "type" table similarly.

The disadvantages are the same for both cases. In many searches, we must join more tables than if we had left the fields where they were. For example, to print a mailing label, we must get the employee's name from the employee table and the city from the zip_code table. Each label thus requires an extra table access, slowing the process considerably. This is the tradeoff for the multi-megabyte savings in disk space. We have sacrificed performance for storage efficiency. In an application study reported by Amdahl Corp. (see the article by Edwards cited below), normalization increased average response time by a factor of 4 and reduced transaction throughput by one-third.

Note, however, that we can reduce or eliminate the performance penalties by clustering the tables. Now additional I/O may be unnecessary.

The fact that we have not even implemented the type table in our example database shows that normal forms (except 1NF) are not essential. The normalization process is, as mentioned, a sort of checklist. Whether one should apply it depends on the tradeoffs among such factors as speed, storage requirements, ease of updating, and comprehensibility. However, if one fails to do so, one should be aware of the risks. An interesting discussion of the practical aspects of normalization appears in J.B. Edwards, "High Performance Without Compromise," *Datamation*, July 1, 1990, pp. 53-58.

If the staff were enlarged to 30 or 40 people, we might want to change the data structure and implement 3NF fully, i.e., create a type table. In practice, of course, it is not easy to change a data structure on which many applications are based. One could make similar objections to forcing the employee table back to 2NF by reinserting the city field.

We can answer the objections in two ways. First, a great advantage of relational databases is that revisions are *not* a major problem. Second, you should never ignore a potential problem; the safest approach is to normalize completely from the start. Any time-independent link that is not isolated is a potential source of errors. We can also avoid much of the domino effect of normalization (or denormalization) by using views in applications rather than actual base tables.

7.6 BCNF

Early in the chapter, we mentioned that instead of normalizing the overall database, we could first set up data elements (entities) as independent "tables" and then normalize them. BCNF (Boyce-Codd Normal Form) takes this approach.

BCNF is not an independent normal form but rather a reinforcement of 3NF, which explains why we do not call it 4NF. BCNF operates on the result of 3NF but has a basis in the unnormalized structure.

It does **not** refer to primary and non-key attributes, but instead uses the concepts of "determinant" and "candidate key". A "candidate key", as mentioned earlier, is a (possibly complex) attribute that can function as a primary key. A "determinant" is an attribute on which others depend. The definition of a table satisfying the BCNF form is that "all determinants must be candidate keys."

To explain this, let us return to our basic table. Note that the attributes employee_no, zip_code, order_no, item_no, and type are determinants because other attributes are determined by them (that is, are uniquely identifiable from them). One may disregard candidate keys that apply only to the entire table. A conversion of the unnormalized structure to BCNF implies that all determinant attributes are made into candidate keys (and, consequently, also into primary keys) in independent tables. The result is to bring the tables into 3NF. Each determinant defines an actual element (an entity), that is, something that should be readily available to make the database useful.

This example is too simple to illustrate how BCNF reinforces 3NF. The motivation for reinforcing 3NF is that table structures having complex candidate keys with overlapping attributes are likely to have attributes in common. The simplified tables are also easier to maintain and more likely to be usable by a wide variety of applications.

7.7 MVD/NF (4NF)

MVD stands for MultiValued Dependencies. The term typically refers to table structures where a dataset or table contains two many-to-many relationships. In our example, for instance, many employees may sell many different items to many different customers. So there are many-to-many relationships between employees and items and between employees and customers.

Assume that the following sales have occurred:

employee_no	item_no	customer_no
17	4014	1002
17	4012	1002
18	4014	1002
18	4014	1004

Some multivalued information is present here. Item_no (4014 and 4012) is multivalued information about employee_no 17, and similarly customer_no (1002 and 1004) is multivalued information about employee_no 18.

This structure is unfortunate, first because it contains redundant information, and second because one does not find the kind of dependencies used previously. Only the primary key exists. We cannot decompose it into a more applicable construction, as we were able to do with previous normal forms. The fully functional dependency (used in converting from 1NF to 2NF) is defined by the existence, for each determinant, of just one value that is functionally dependent on it. However, the construction above has no functional dependencies because many pieces of multivalued information (several item_no's and customer_no's) are linked to the determinant employee_no. In principle, we are reduced to working on the unnormalized table. The unique relationship between a primary key (determinant) and dependent values that could be used in other normal forms does not apply here.

Obviously, we can solve the problem by simple projection so each MVD appears in its own table: table_1 (employee_no, item_no) and table_2 (employee_no, customer_no). But instead of using the functional dependencies in decomposition (all attributes contribute to the determinant), we must use the new construction, that is, the multivalued dependencies:

employee_no—> —>item_no

employee_no—> —>customer_no

Next, we form two new tables, tab_1 and tab_2, both representing many-to-many relationships.

tab1	employee_no	item_no
	17	4014
	17	4012
	18	4014
tab2	employee_no	customer_no
	17	1002
	18	1002
	18	1004

In contrast to the functional dependencies (where a value corresponds to a given determinant), here there are no determinants except the combination of attributes.

The difficulties associated with MVD's are insignificant. After all, their structural characteristics have already disappeared when we remove the repeating groups in converting the unnormalized structure to the table in 1NF.

7.8 PJ/NF (5NF)

5NF is also called **Projection/Join Normal Form** (PJ/NF). We have previously mentioned that a projection can always decompose a table into two new tables without any loss of information. In all cases where we did this, the opposite is also true: we can join the two tables again without any loss of information.

However, this rule has exceptions. Some structures are so irregular that we cannot decompose them into two tables without loss of information, whereas we can decompose them successfully into three or more tables.

No example occurs among the material presented so far in this book, so we constructed the table below to illustrate the point. It has records for each item that an employee has sold to a particular customer. Its original source is Date's widely used textbook on database systems. The database contains the following records:

tab_1		
Employee_no	Item_no	Customer_no
17	4014	1002
17	4019	1003
19	4014	1003
17	4014	1003

We can make the following projections:

tab_2		tab_3	
E	I	I	C
17	4014	4014	1002
17	4019	4019	1003
19	4014	4014	1003

As with previous projections, we should now be able to join the two tables to form the original one. However, if we join tab_2 and tab_3 over V, the result is:

tab_5			
E	I	C	
17	4014	1002	
17	4014	1003	
17	4019	1003	
19	4014	1002	does not exist in tab_1
19	4014	1003	

We can also make the following projection from tab_1:

tab_4	
C	E
1002	17
1003	17
1003	19

To restore the original table, we must join tab_5 and tab_4 (over C and E). In other words, we cannot project tab_1 into two tables without errors, but we can project it into three tables in a valid way.

The problem is not to resolve the anomaly because all we must do is make the necessary projections. The challenge is rather to find the anomalies. In most cases involving fifth normal form, the problems disappear during conversions to earlier normal forms.

8

Integrity

Chapter 7 described normalization, the process of specifying the most reasonable way to divide the database into tables based on knowing what their contents mean and how they are related. You can implement it by isolating useful relationships in their own separate tables. The result is to reduce redundancy, simplify updating, and make data more readily accessible for a wide range of applications. The focus is on the structural aspects of logical database design.

This chapter describes the requirements and methods for ensuring that data is initially correct and remains so. The common feature of all errors is that they violate the database's integrity. The term "integrity" implies both internal and external consistency. The database should have neither internal contradictions nor discrepancies with its external sources. A breach of integrity thus means the presence of inconsistent data or connections. For instance, we may have two different Zip Codes for the same employee or a single Zip Code that is erroneous or nonexistent.

Errors may occur in many places and as a result of many different actions. Since they affect integrity, before discussing them, we will briefly describe the three types of integrity, namely entity, semantic, and referential.

Entity integrity refers to the data in a single table. The name comes from the common use of "entity" to mean a real-world element such as a customer. It is a breach of entity integrity to fail to find an established customer in the database. Section 8.2 discusses this further.

Semantic integrity refers to whether the entered data has the proper form or range of values. If an entry specifies that Smith earns B600 or 16 (instead of 1600), it is a breach of semantic integrity. Section 8.2 treats this subject further.

Referential integrity describes the relationships among tables. It is a breach of referential integrity if, for example, an entry specifies customer 9000 but no such customer number exists in the database. Section 8.3 treats referential integrity further.

Errors can arise in any database configuration, but single-user systems are relatively robust because only one person works with them (establishing their structures, entering or deleting data, etc.). Thus a single person is responsible for database integrity. Others may use the database but **not at the same time.**

In multiuser systems, i.e., shared databases, several users (or programs) can work with the same data **at the same time.** Now there is a new source of errors not present in single-user systems. Here errors may occur simply because of simultaneous access. If updates do not occur sequentially, some may be lost. The result is a breach of database integrity, but the error is not the fault of a user but rather of the system itself. Chapter 11 discusses the subject further.

Another type of error that can occur with any database is a system error. Such errors arise when, for example, power fails before all changes have been saved, or the data disk malfunctions or fails. It is surely a breach of integrity if data cannot be accessed. Chapter 11 describes typical problems and solutions.

8.1 Entity Integrity

Each record in a table that contains real-world data is often said to be associated with an "entity". The table may consist of actual data or may just specify relationships among other tables. The term "entity integrity" means that each record must contain what it is meant to contain. It must be consistent internally and with its purpose. A primary key must exist that identifies it uniquely. To have a table with no primary key makes no sense, as its elements would not be uniquely retrievable. A primary key with duplicate values causes similar problems.

Even though a table with no primary key is useless, you can, practically speaking, establish one. SQL does not support the concept of primary key as a "semantic" feature (i.e., referring to its contents or meaning) of a table, not a structural feature. The lack of a primary key restricts the usefulness of the data, as searches or statistical analysis may be meaningless if records exist that are not uniquely identifiable.

The DBA can use two elements of SQL to help ensure (but not guarantee!) the existence of a primary key:

- Specify the attributes that form the key as NOT NULL during the definition of the table structure. NOT NULL is a necessary feature for a primary key.

- Force the establishment of a UNIQUE index using the combination of attributes that form the primary key.

Beginning with SQL/DS Version 2, Release 2, IBM has included the primary key as a clause in the CREATE TABLE command. A typical example is:

```
CREATE TABLE orders
(order_no INTEGER NOT NULL,
customer_no INTEGER NOT NULL,
employee_no INTEGER,
received DATE NOT NULL,
shipped DATE,
PRIMARY KEY (order_no,customer_no));
```

The DBMS establishes and automatically maintains a unique index for the primary key.

However, except in SQL/DS, the DBA must establish the necessary indexes. The ANSI standard does not mention primary key.

8.2 Semantic Integrity

The absence of a primary key is not the only problem that leads to violations of entity integrity. When discussing normalization to 3NF, we mentioned that the relationship between the determinant "type" (employee type) and "base_pay" was a transitive dependence. Therefore, we should isolate it in a separate table.

We have not done this. Although the database structure is correct, nothing can prevent a user from making erroneous entries or updates. An example is giving an employee of type M a base pay of 1600 in one record and 1700 in another. Implementing full 3NF would make this mistake impossible, as there would be a single table containing the base pay for each employee type. Here we are dealing with a semantic integrity problem related to the contents of individual data elements.

SQL does not support semantic integrity checks, and they can be implemented only partially via control routines in embedded SQL (see Chapter 9). When dealing with numerical data such as base pay or number of working hours, they would involve entering it into ordinary program variables and validating it. An example is checking that the number of weekly hours worked does not exceed 40. No test can guard against the user entering 18 or 37 instead of the actual 38. Most other types of data also require checking by control routines. Some data can, however, be validated without considering its contents. An example is the self-checks included in some credit card numbers and identification tags. A validity check can guarantee that a number is valid but not that it is correct.

Relational database theory includes a concept not implemented in SQL that can help solve the problem. The concept is "domains", the ranges of permissible or possible values for a field. The concept is semantic in nature. Figure 8-1 shows typical fields and their associated domains. SQL does not allow for explicit domain specifications or the narrower idea of enumerated types (such as seasons, months, or colors) supported in many procedural languages (e.g., C and Pascal).

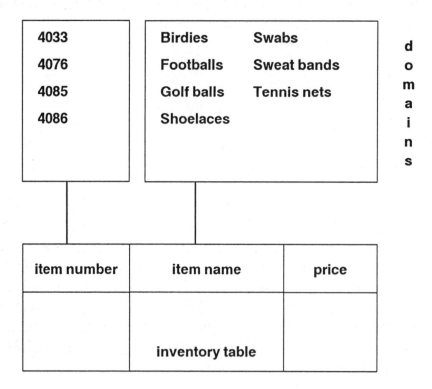

Figure 8-1. Field values and their associated domains.

With specified domains, the procedure to ensure semantic integrity works as follows. Define tables of the valid elements for checking purposes. Do not let the DBMS enter a transaction such as

```
INSERT INTO employees (last_name,street,zip_code)
VALUES("Smith","Lake Avenue","34765")
```

permanently into the database **until** it verifies that all the data values are in the corresponding tables.

The commands INSERT (and UPDATE) would thus behave as though they contained the following conditions:

```
IF EXISTS
SELECT * FROM domain_last_name
WHERE last_name = "Smith"
AND SELECT * FROM domain_street
WHERE street = "Lake Avenue"
THEN INSERT INTO employees...
```

We can, in principle, handle any data in this way, but, practically speaking, domains for such items as names and addresses are unmanageably large. Simple table lookups can do the job for small domains. Larger ones require rules about combinations and the applicability of operators. For example, it should be permissible to perform "SELECT base_pay * tax_rate" and "SELECT first_name + last_name" but not "SELECT base_pay - tax_rate" or "SELECT first_name - last_name".

A simple way to help reduce typing errors is to substitute numerical codes for common values. In particular, we can use codes instead of strings. For example, consider the many different errors users can make when entering an item description such as "Skipping rope (8 feet)". They could type the wrong letters, omit or transpose characters, or enter capital letters instead of lowercase, a bracket or brace instead of a parenthesis, too few or too many spaces, etc. Minor errors lead to misleading statistics, reports, and other information. Surely just specifying the item as "16" is faster and less error-prone. Of course, the numerical codes are meaningless, and the user must look them up somewhere. But the results will be a great improvement over having people type item names such as "accordion", "frequency synthesizer", or "acetaminophen".

Another way to avoid serious errors is to establish views of individual tables and be careful who has GRANT UPDATE and GRANT

INSERT capabilities. Still another solution for small domains involves using tools such as form and report generators.

8.3 Referential Integrity

Referential integrity refers to consistency **among** tables. They may form a hierarchy in which some control others ("own" them) or are subordinate ("owned"). Obviously, a table may be subordinate to some tables and superior to others (a middle status in the "pecking order"). An example is the order table which is owned by the customer and employee tables, but is itself the owner of the order_specs table. We often call the dependent table a "child" and the one on which it depends the "parent". Be careful—tables may have modern-style families with many parents and shared children.

Here we must introduce the concept of "foreign key". It is an attribute in an owned table that presupposes the existence of a primary key value in another table (the owner). One might say that the relationship between the two keys establishes a dependency between the two tables. An owned table can have multiple foreign keys, and the foreign keys can be compound and can include NULL attributes.

In the database example, Figure 8-2 shows the dependencies. An arrow between a foreign key and a primary key means "requires an exact match".

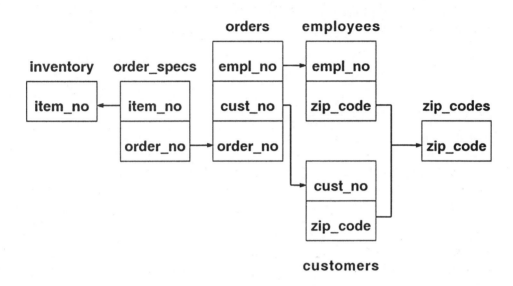

Figure 8-2. Relationships between primary key and foreign keys.

The existence of primary and foreign keys implies requirements when the user deletes a record from an owner table. To preserve integrity, the user must either delete records from the dependent tables or observe certain precautions. Furthermore, one can only add a record to the dependent table if the owner contains a primary key with its value. For example, suppose we delete a record from the order table. Perhaps the items were out of stock or the shipment was lost or returned. Here we should also delete the corresponding records from the order_specs table. After all, if the order is gone, its details should vanish with it. We describe the process as "cascaded deletion" (DELETE CASCADES). If it does not occur, the database would no longer be consistent as order specifications would exist without a corresponding order.

However, if we delete a record from the employee table (which owns the order table), we cannot allow cascaded deletion. Otherwise, information on customers' balances would disappear as well. Instead, we use "restricted deletion" (DELETE RESTRICTED), which leads to the following analysis.

If the employee has no orders in the order table, he or she can be deleted with no problems. "Good night, sweet prince - you never brought any paying customers to the castle drama series anyway." However, if the employee **has** orders, nothing happens. You must remember that the intended deletion (an employee) has not actually occurred, and the integrity of the database has been lost. Some administrative action is necessary.

Another possibility is to assign the foreign key the value NULL (DELETE NULLIFIES), provided that the attribute definition allows it. This, too, requires further steps.

Similar problems occur if you update records in a table owned by others (updating the primary key). Changing an employee_no in the employee table **should** update all records (in other tables) involving the employee in question.

SQL/DS Version 2, Release 2 implements the following syntax:

```
CREATE TABLE orders
(order_no INTEGER NOT NULL,
customer_no INTEGER NOT NULL,
employee_no INTEGER NOT NULL,
received DATE,
shipped DATE,
PRIMARY KEY (order_no),
FOREIGN KEY orders_customers(customer_no)
REFERENCES customers
ON DELETE RESTRICT
FOREIGN KEY orders_employees(employee_no)
REFERENCES employees
ON DELETE CASCADES)
```

The extensions specify the relationships among the individual tables (referential integrity), and have the following meanings:

PRIMARY KEY indicates that the field order_no is the primary key in the table. The DBMS establishes a unique index on the field. PRIMARY KEY can also be added to an existing table with the command ALTER TABLE ADD PRIMARY KEY. This works only if the primary key in the existing table has no NULL values. The primary key may be removed, deactivated, or reactivated.

The FOREIGN KEY clause indicates that the field customer_no in the order table is a foreign key that refers to (REFERENCES) the customer table. The reference itself is called orders_customers, and the name is used to remove, activate, or deactivate it.

The creation of the reference (orders_customers) presumes that customer_no in the customer table is the primary key. So no order can be entered unless its recipient is already in the customer table. Another consequence is that you cannot change this field in the order table to a value that does not exist in the customer table.

ON DELETE RESTRICT refers to what must happen if we delete a record from the customer table. RESTRICT makes it impossible. It also means that a customer_no cannot be changed in a way that would violate referential integrity.

Alternatives to ON DELETE RESTRICT are the following:

ON DELETE CASCADES: If we delete the primary key in the customer table, all corresponding records in the order table are also deleted.

ON DELETE SET NULL: If we delete the primary key in the customer table, all corresponding records in the order table are assigned the value NULL in the field (unless it is defined as NOT NULL).

The SQL/DS implementation has restrictions and shortcomings. Nevertheless, it represents great progress and is a precedent for other database programs. Finally, we should note that the ANSI standard includes neither PRIMARY KEY nor FOREIGN KEY.

The reason for this long discussion of ensuring referential integrity is that it can significantly reduce the risk of introducing inconsistency. The implementation of primary and foreign key clauses will only work in some cases. Similar restrictions apply to any procedural element introduced into a non-procedural language. However, the innovation can prevent relationships among the tables from being completely lost.

We have already mentioned a situation in which this feature is of little use, namely when an employee is deleted. Neither RESTRICT nor CASCADES can handle the task (SET NULL is illegal) because the employee **must** be deleted, and the records in the order table must be saved.

What is lacking is a message to the user forcing him or her to decide whether to save the employee's orders (either under another name or in a historical table created for that purpose). Another procedural element is required.

We should also note that creating views can help **prevent** inconsistencies in databases. A characteristic of views formed by joining tables is that no updates, deletions, or additions are allowed. This does not support the implementation of referential integrity, but it does prevent problems from arising.

8.4 Concurrency

The problems treated above may appear in all types of databases (single-user and multiuser or distributed systems). However, errors are more likely in multiuser systems. First, the database is typically more complex, i.e., more tables refer to one another. Second, there are more users to make mistakes. However, other problems may arise, caused not by the way users treat tables but by the way the DBMS tries to handle multiple users. We refer to the overall issue as the problem of **concurrency**. But before describing it in detail, we must introduce the concept of a "transaction".

Transactions

A "transaction" is a sequence of operations or events in the database. The basic operations in question are SELECT, INSERT, UPDATE, and DELETE.

The simplest possible transaction consists of three phases:

- Fetch

- Update

- Commit or rollback

The fetch phase involves locating the data and moving it to the appropriate area of memory. The update phase involves changing the records. The changes do **not** affect the "original" data but rather a "log file" that then contains both the original and the changed data. The transaction command itself is saved in a "transaction log file". Chapter 11 describes log files and transaction log files further.

In the last phase, the alternatives are either a COMMIT or a ROLLBACK command. Either the program or the user can issue a COMMIT command. It can also be issued implicitly when the SET AUTOCOMMIT ON of the control system is active, or it can be done by the DBMS performing so-called "synchronizations" at certain intervals (as described in a later section). The result of a COMMIT is to write the contents of the log file (the changed records) into the physical database, thus making the changes permanent. The log file does not change, as it must serve as a backup if the data disk is destroyed or becomes unusable.

Just as with COMMIT, a ROLLBACK can be issued explicitly by users or implicitly by the system. The latter happens when an error occurs during a transaction. ROLLBACK means that the changes do **not** become permanent. The contents of the log file are not written into the physical database.

In summation, a transaction ends with a COMMIT or a ROLL-BACK. Its successor can then begin. We describe a "synchronization point" as a point at which a transaction is either committed or discarded (rolled back). Note that a transaction is not necessarily just a "fetch-update-save" process, but can be an entire sequence of operations. In other words, the log file may not just reflect a single update but may involve many commands (INSERT, DELETE, or UPDATE). The contents may be written into the database at times defined by:

- The issuance of an explicit COMMIT/ROLLBACK.

- An implicit COMMIT/ROLLBACK.

- A system synchronization point.

- An automatic COMMIT of all changes that occurs when work with the database ends (logoff).

In the following examples, we assume that AUTOCOMMIT is OFF, so the user or the applications program must issue a COMMIT to register changes. There are risks in this approach, as the log file grows because of unsaved changes. If something goes wrong or a ROLLBACK is issued, the contents of unsaved (uncommitted) changes are lost. A ROLLBACK cannot (thank goodness!) be rolled back. The system lacks any further ability to postpone an action.

The fact that we may regard the contents of the log file since the last COMMIT or ROLLBACK as a single transaction is very important because it gives us a way to ensure integrity. The following two situations are examples:

- The user plans to delete a record (it has been annulled) but accidentally deletes the wrong one.

- A new order has been received which we intend to put into the order table. It will require several new records in the order_specs table. Until the new records are entered, the database is inconsistent because an order exists without some of its contents being specified. The person entering the new records into order_specs may err (e.g., enter the wrong quantity, wrong order number, etc.).

The solution in both cases is to issue a ROLLBACK and start over.

The user seldom issues commands directly. Most often, a screen display instructs the user to enter values. He or she does not have to worry about how many tables are changed or about database consistency. The underlying program handles such matters. The following pseudo-program (Figure 8-3) shows what happens. Here we have embedded SQL commands in an ordinary high level language (see Chapter 9).

```
print('Enter order number:');read(order_no)
print('Enter customer number:');read(customer_no)
print('Enter employee number:');read(employee_no)
EXEC SQL INSERT INTO CUSTOMERS
    VALUES(:order_no,:customer_no,:employee_no)
if SQLCODE < 0 goto error_handler
continue = 'Yes'
while continue = 'Yes' do
print('Enter order number:');read(order_no)
```

```
print('Enter item number:');read(item_no)
print('Enter quantity:');read(quantity)
EXEC SQL INSERT INTO order_specs
    VALUES(:order_no, :item_no, :number)
if SQLCODE <> 0 goto error_handler
print('Must several be entered (Yes/No)?')
read(continue)
endwhile
EXEC SQL COMMIT
:error_handler
print('An error occurred, please start over.')
EXEC SQL ROLLBACK
```

Figure 8-3. Solution of the referential integrity problem using a programming language.

When several tables are being changed simultaneously, errors may occur. The program then branches to an **error handler** which prints a message and does a ROLLBACK. The result is to delete the order and its specifications. The process then must start over. The advantage of having the COMMIT command at the end and thus combining the individual transactions is that updating is an all-or-none process. So the database's integrity is sure to remain intact. If something goes wrong, extra work must be done, but this is preferable to creating an unknown number of order_specs records that the user would have to find and delete later.

The program tests the value SQLCODE which we will explain in Chapter 9. The system maintains SQLCODE, and a negative value indicates an error serious enough to stop the program.

The Concurrency Problem

The concurrency problem arises when several transactions operate on the same data or on interdependent data. The following example (Figure 8-4) illustrates the situation. A clerk receives an order for 12 basketballs from a customer. There are 34 in stock. The stock must be reduced to reflect the sale. At the same time, a supplier delivers 50 new balls, requiring another stock update. The result should be a stock of 34-12+50 or 72 balls.

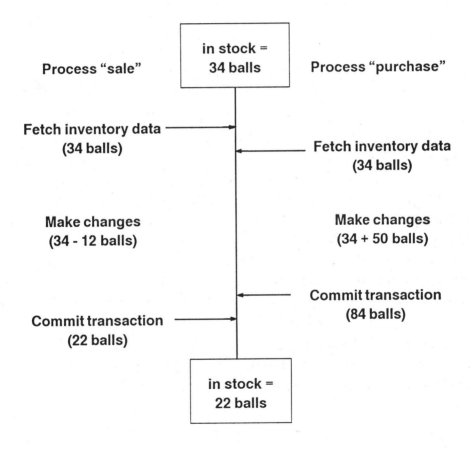

Figure 8-4. Two simultaneous updates of the stock table.

If the vertical axis is time, we see both transactions operating on the same data. However, the interaction causes an error because one result (the sale) overwrites the other (the purchase). We need a general, flexible way for one transaction to force another to wait.

Locks

When multiple transactions try to work on the same data simultaneously, the result may be inconsistency. The solution is to apply a "lock" to the data.

Such problems occur only in on-line systems. Batch systems usually handle transactions sequentially, so lost updates cannot occur.

Locks are marks put on records or other units of the database, such as an entire table, a certain number of bytes, or a logically defined part (see Chapter 2). They are set and removed automatically during transactions. We refer to the standard method as *two-phase locking*.

During the first phase, the DBMS evaluates the transaction and locks all records that are involved. If there are many such records, leaving them all locked throughout the process would probably delay many transactions. To avoid or reduce such delays, we introduce a second phase that starts when some changes have been made. The DBMS can then unlock records that are no longer in use, so other transactions may access them. Two-phase locking thus means that unlocking occurs in stages rather than all at once. There is an obvious drawback, however, if the entire transaction fails and must be rolled back. The DBMS must keep track of all events so that it can cancel them if necessary.

Though locking works automatically, the user can decide which type of lock to apply and its extent or granularity. The granularity can be columns, tables, or dataspaces (a collection of tables, see Chapter 11).

Basically, there are three types of locks: "exclusive locks", "shared locks", and "wait locks". Oracle also has a "shared update lock". All operate as two-phase locks.

An exclusive lock means that no other transaction can change the data. Another term for it is a "write lock". No other transaction can lock the data or even read it. After all, the reader could not be sure that the locking transaction had finished its changes.

The following command sets an exclusive lock:

```
LOCK TABLE name IN EXCLUSIVE MODE
```

How extensively a lock applies determines how the work on the database proceeds. If it applies to an entire database, all other users are prevented from working with tables even if they are not immediately being updated. However, the user can limit the command by issuing

```
LOCK DBSPACE space_name IN SHARED MODE
```

The advantage is that the work goes faster.

A lock at the table level is more limited but may still delay searches involving two tables. The user of one table must wait until someone else has finished the search on the other table if it is also locked. Transactions that operate on data with an exclusive lock must wait in line, equipped with a "numbered" wait lock.

"Shared locks" allow other users to read the data but not change it. Other transactions may also put a shared lock on the same data, but a request for an exclusive or shared update lock will cause a wait lock.

A shared update lock is Oracle's version of IBM's lock on columns, which cannot be set inactively but only by defining a public dbspace. Such a lock can be set in two ways in Oracle, either explicitly by issuing the command

```
LOCK TABLE table_name IN SHARED UPDATE MODE
```

or implicitly with a command such as:

```
SELECT * FROM table_name WHERE field3 > 76
FOR UPDATE OF field1, field2
```

This puts an exclusive lock on field1 and field2 in records where field3 is greater than 76.

Wait locks are set implicitly when a transaction is trying to set a lock in vain. They have priority according to the FIFO principle (first-in, first-out). The lock that has been waiting the longest is handled first.

The matrix in Table 8-1 illustrates the interplay among different types of locks. The answers indicate whether a particular type (determined by the row) can be obtained when another type (determined by the column) is already in effect. For example, if an exclusive lock is in effect, no other lock can be obtained. Hence, all answers in the EXCLUSIVE column are "no". On the other hand, another shared lock can be obtained even when one is already in effect, so the answer in the SHARED row and SHARED column is "yes".

Table 8-1. Interplay Among Different Types of Locks.

LOCK TO BE OBTAINED	LOCK ALREADY SET		
	SHARED	SHARED UPDATE	EXCLUSIVE
SHARED	yes	no	no
SHARED UPDATE	no	yes	no
EXCLUSIVE	no	no	no

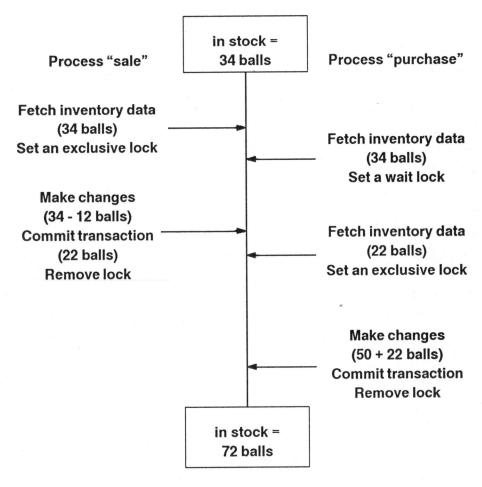

Figure 8-5. Two simultaneous updates of the stock table with locks.

Figure 8-5 shows what happens when we add locks to the process of Figure 8-4. Transaction "sale" first identifies the records to be updated. When it finds them, it sets a lock, forcing transaction "purchase" to wait until it is done. "Purchase" waits until the lock manager removes the lock. This occurs when "sale" implicitly or explicitly finishes, either with the COMMIT or the ROLLBACK command. Next, "purchase" reads the size of the inventory. When it is ready to update, it sets an exclusive lock. It now reads the inventory size and adds 50 to it. The result is the correct one, 72 balls.

Deadlocks

A "deadlock" occurs when one transaction is impatiently waiting for another to finish, and at the same time the other one is equally impatiently waiting for it. In other words, the two are locked in a deadly embrace. Or, to put it less seriously, an endless Alphonse and Gaston act.

An example (see Figure 8-6) is the following. Suppose transactions A and B both must update the order_specs and order tables. Transaction A starts with order_specs, B with orders. The result is that both transactions wait, and neither has priority because both are partly done.

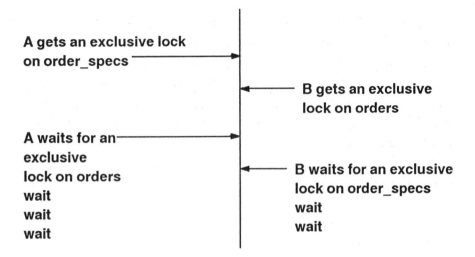

Figure 8-6. Example deadlock situation.

One way to remove a deadlock is for the transaction manager to "back out" of one transaction. The choice could be the one that started last or the one that had done the least when the deadlock occurred. To back out means to save the contents of the transaction and remove the changes that it has already made to the tables. When the first transaction finishes, the other one can proceed (like a disgruntled motorist who must wait for a crossing gate to rise or a drawbridge to lower).

Locks (types, uses, and scopes) are program dependent and many variations exist in practice.

8.5 Recovery

The preceding section on concurrency gives examples of various error conditions. All were situations that the system itself can handle. However, more basic and thus also more extensive errors may occur, and for that reason DBMSs typically have elaborate "recovery" routines. Their function is to salvage a database after an error. The usual situation is one in which the database ends up in an inconsistent state but no one knows **how** inconsistent it is or **where** the inconsistency is located.

Backup

Typical errors requiring recovery routines are global system errors caused by power loss or disk damage. Here a backup routine is **necessary** but may not be sufficient to restore the database's integrity. Backup routines copy the database as it is here and now. No matter how frequently backups occur, there may still be uncommitted transactions that they do not include.

In many instances, we cannot make backups of the entire database frequently because of time constraints. Backups are, therefore, often only made daily (e.g., at night) or weekly. If a global system error occurs after a backup copy has been made, the backup can always be used, and the database can be recovered. It is then consistent but not up-to-date. Transactions may have occurred since the last backup. A log of events in the database can be used to correct much of the damage.

The Log

A database consists of three elements:

- A directory that contains control information about the database and its structure, and about the relationship between its logical and physical organizations.

- Log files that record all changes.

- Data files that hold the contents after the last COMMIT command.

Backup or archiving is a necessary but not sufficient safety measure to ensure database integrity. What is missing is a **continuing** registry of current events in the database. The log performs this function, and as it is much smaller physically than the entire database, a daily backup of it can provide a reasonable safety net. We also must track transactions as they occur. This is the job of the "transaction log".

Let us briefly consider an example of using all three components to recover a database. We use **the backup, the log**, and a **transaction log**.

Suppose that on Thursday you notice that the data disks have become unreadable. Perhaps you should not have used them as Frisbees during the midweek picnic. After a brief fit of sobbing and swearing, you start the recovery process. First you enter the last backup (from Friday), restoring the database's state at that time. With it as a basis, you run the log (actually its backup) from Monday to restore all transactions from that day. Next, you run the logs from Tuesday and Wednesday to restore the state on Wednesday evening.

All that is missing are the changes that occurred on Thursday. Before we recover this data, we must explain briefly how standard database operations are performed.

A "block" or "page" is the unit of data transfer between mass storage and RAM. It is typically a few thousand bytes. One block can thus hold many records from a table. When the DBMS asks, for example, to update a certain record in a table, the computer copies the entire block containing it to RAM.

Not all RAM is available for data manipulation, because the operating system uses some of it for **buffers**. Some buffers contain information about the directory (where tables are stored), some hold data waiting to be used, and still others hold recently used data blocks.

Startup parameters usually control the number and size of buffers. Such parameters have a major impact on database performance, because of their role in system optimization. The more buffers there are and the larger they are, the more likely it is that the data one wants to manipulate is already in RAM. The user then saves valuable time that would otherwise go to disk I/O. The disadvantage is that buffers reduce the amount of RAM available for data manipulation. When a user issues, for example, an UPDATE command, the DBMS performs the following steps:

1.   It checks the buffers to see whether the data is already present. If so, all it must do is update the buffers. No slow disk operations are necessary. This is like finding the papers you need already on your desk rather than in unmarked cartons in the basement.

2.   If not, the DBMS checks the buffers of directory information to see whether they contain the needed addresses. If so, it will use them to access the blocks. This is not as good as having the data itself, but at least you know where it is.

3.   If not, the DBMS checks the directory file and loads the relevant address blocks into a buffer. It then uses the addresses to find the desired data blocks on the disk.

4.   The operating system now loads the data blocks into RAM. Or rather, it puts them in buffers.

The process described above means that the DBMS is actually changing the buffers, not the database itself. So the database (the physically stored data) is seldom current because recent changes are in the buffers, waiting to be written to disk. Note that if a power loss occurs, the contents of the buffers disappear. Perhaps such an event occurred on the Thursday mentioned above. Someone returning a bit groggy from a potent carrot juice lunch tripped over the power cord, dislodging it.

When the DBMS fetches a block, it puts the contents both into the buffers and into what we call a "before image file". SQL/DS uses the term "shadow pages" for a similar feature. The file holds the original records **before** they were fetched for manipulation.

When the DBMS makes the changes, it writes them both into the buffer (and later into the database) and into a so-called "after image file". It contains the updated records after the changes have been made.

We may regard the database as a "linked list" (Figure 8-7) in which an individual record (or block) is connected to its successor via a pointer. When a record is changed, the new version is saved in the after image and a new pointer is created, linking the before image to it. A similar pointer connects the after image chain back to the database. The old chain of "before image" records still exists and can be used if needed.

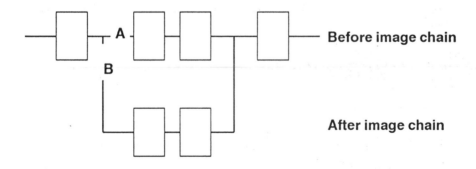

Figure 8-7. Log registers changes in the database.

When records are changed (without a COMMIT or ROLL-BACK), the new versions form the basis of other updates. Thus if, for example, employee 14's monthly pay increases from $1500 to $1600 and then later is raised again by $100, his or her pay will be $1700 even though no COMMIT occurred.

A COMMIT enters the latest transaction into the database. It makes the DBMS store the after image file permanently. The pointer chain is broken at point A in Figure 8-7 so only the new records remain in it.

In the event of a ROLLBACK, the pointers return to the before image chain. The pointer chain is broken at B and permanently established at A. Employee 14 returns to a base pay of $1500. Too bad that inflation is never rolled back accordingly.

Now let us return to where this digression started (wherever that was!). The latest transactions, which are not in the archived log files, lie in the before and after images. You can find Thursday's work in them. The only problem is that the buffer containing the changed but not yet committed data is in an unstable state, because the data is untraceable until it has been transferred to the after image file.

The last point we make about how the DBMS works is to describe the concept of a "checkpoint record" and the transaction log. The system automatically performs regular checkpoints (after certain time intervals or more typically when the log file has increased by a certain number of new blocks).

The DBMS handles a checkpoint as follows:

- It writes a checkpoint record into the log. The record indicates when the checkpoint started (a "time stamp") and holds the status of ongoing transactions.

- It stops all ongoing transactions and other database activity. New transactions cannot begin.

- It makes the contents of all buffers permanent by writing them into physical storage.

- It updates the log with changes that might not yet be committed.

- It frees the log contents of before images (shadow pages).

A checkpoint is a key element in recovery because it indicates a time when the database is consistent, or more precisely, when the **combination** of the database, the log file, and the checkpoint record is consistent. So even though the log has not been backed up yet today, we can still recover the database by "reading" the log up to the checkpoint. The system maintains both an overall log and a transaction log, registering the contents of individual transactions. If we issue

```
INSERT INTO order...
```

the transaction log contains a record that might say: 1988-01-20-12-:16:45,120:INSERT INTO order... The transaction log records every command issued and when it was performed.

Figure 8-8 (taken from Date's *Introduction to Database Systems*) shows a sequence of transactions occurring before a serious error. We can interpret it as follows.

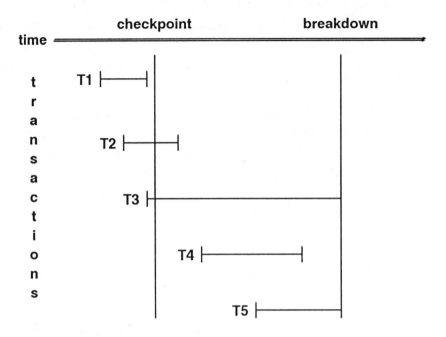

Figure 8-8. Recovery from a system error.

Transaction T1 finishes before the checkpoint. It is, therefore, executed before the breakdown and is not affected by it.

Transaction T2 starts before the checkpoint but does not finish before it. T2 appears in a checkpoint record as in progress. It finishes before breakdown and may be regarded as "probably successful". We say "probably" because we do not know if a ROLLBACK would have occurred if an attempt had been made to commit it. The before image of the affected records is registered.

T3 starts before the checkpoint but does not finish before the breakdown. It must be regarded as unsuccessful. The transaction is registered in a checkpoint record.

T4 starts after the checkpoint and finishes, but is not committed before the breakdown. We should regard it as "probably successful".

T5 starts after the checkpoint and must be considered unsuccessful because we do not know what would have happened if it had run its course.

When the system is started again after the breakdown, the checkpoint records (transaction log) will indicate which transactions were in progress and what they were doing at the time of the breakdown. Its status will be as follows:

- The log for T2 will include both a "start transaction" and a commit.

- The log for T3 will include a "start transaction" but no commit.

- The log for T4 will include both a "start transaction" and a commit.

- The log for T5 will include a "start transaction" but no commit.

When a checkpoint occurs, the system writes a time stamp into the log. The recovery process can reestablish transactions by reading the log until it encounters the last time stamp. From there, it reads "forward" to find transactions that can be redone. In Figure 8-8, this means T2 and T4. The others (T3 and T5) must have their work deleted. After the reading reaches the breakdown, it starts backward and undoes T3 and T5. Backward reading continues until the time stamp after which the contents of the log file are performed. With the exception of T3 and T5, the database can be reestablished.

9

Embedded SQL

SQL is a a non-procedural language (that is, one that specifies what results to obtain rather than how to obtain them). It operates on "sets" or tables rather than on individual data items, as most procedural languages do. Users specify what they want done by describing the information they need. They do not tell the computer how to conduct searches, but rather let the DBMS determine the best way to produce the desired outcome.

One well-known PC database management system actually advises users facing syntax problems to "try doing it in English first". The idea behind SQL is that its syntax should be close enough to ordinary English for untrained users to employ it. In practice, a statement such as

```
SELECT company_name FROM customers
```

is much more like an English sentence than are its FORTRAN or Pascal program equivalents.

We do not claim that SQL is user-friendly. Like other programming languages, it is not intended for **end** users, but rather for applications programmers and database administrators.

To work with SQL effectively, you must know:

- Its syntax (which is English-like).

- The structures of the individual tables.

- The connections between tables.

- The permissible ranges and data types of individual fields and combinations.

But in spite of SQL's features and English-like syntax, it has limitations. They are the result of its set-based outlook and its non-procedural form. SQL's weaknesses include:

- Inability to handle user interaction (the user interface).

- Limited provisions for maintaining integrity (particularly referential but also semantic).

There are two ways to work around these weaknesses. One is to enhance SQL with procedural elements, a process that will take a long time under standards committee rules and schedules. Note, however, that much current work is aimed at adding features that make procedural elements unnecessary. For example, to aid in maintaining database integrity (see Chapter 8), SQL/DS has, as mentioned, added primary and foreign keys to the CREATE command, thus solving some problems.

The other method is to embed SQL statements in common general purpose programming languages. This is the subject of the current chapter. A final example shows SQL embedded in a program written in the popular C language.

The programming language in which one embeds SQL is called the "host language". Typical examples such as Pascal, C, and FORTRAN are procedure-oriented. All statements are translated and executed sequentially (one after the other). For example, the following program consists of a block of three sequentially executed statements inside "begin" and "end" indicators.

```
begin
a = 5
b = a + 20
print b
end
```

Like SQL, procedural languages have advantages and disadvantages. Their major disadvantage in database applications is that they are organized around instruction sequences and individual data items rather than sets.

The procedural approach has the following advantages:

- User interaction is easy to program. For example, one can readily print prompts such as

```
"Enter the name of the employee:"
```

- One can easily validate data entries through statements such
  as

```
"IF weekly_hours > 45 THEN DO something"
```

- One can insure the integrity of the database, as shown in
  Figure 8-3.

Procedural and non-procedural languages thus complement each
other well in database applications. The strengths of each approach
exactly counter the other's weaknesses.

9.1 Pre-Compilation

SQL statements cannot, of course, simply be placed in programs
written in a procedural language. A program with both procedural
and non-procedural elements must be handled differently than one
that has just one type. A special stage must separate the two types of
statements. We call it a **pre-compiler,** as it runs ahead of the actual
compiler. Note that you can only embed SQL statements in a language for which a pre-compiler is available. Such tools exist only for
certain combinations of SQL implementations, database systems,
procedural language compilers, and operating systems. The availability is thus language, software, and hardware dependent. And it is
changing as new languages (particularly Ada, C, and C++) gain wide
acceptance. Languages for which pre-compilers are often available
include Ada, assembly, C, COBOL, FORTRAN, Pascal, and PL/I.
Embedded SQL is also available for some procedural database languages such as Ashton-Tate's dBASE.

An embedded SQL program consists of three parts: a "declaration part", an "include part", and a "program part". Program 9-1, which deletes a record from the customer table, shows the division.

```
EXEC SQL BEGIN DECLARE SECTION
integer cno
EXEC SQL END DECLARE SECTION

EXEC SQL INCLUDE SQLCA

begin
    print('Enter number of customer to delete:')
    read(cno)
    EXEC SQL DELETE FROM customers
    WHERE customer_no = :cno
    print('customer',cno,' removed from database')
end
```

Program 9-1. Delete a Customer Record Using Embedded SQL.

We will explain the individual parts of the program later. Note that we are writing examples in an unspecified high level language that resembles both C and Pascal.

Before the computer can execute Program 9-1, which includes both procedural and non-procedural statements, several stages of translation are necessary. The two languages differ so much that no direct connection between them is possible, hence we cannot create a single executable module. Instead, we create two independent units. One, the host, controls the sequence of operations. When the programs run, it calls the other part, consisting of DBMS operations, as required.

The first stage, therefore, is to separate the elements of the two languages. As we noted, the pre-compiler does this. It separates the host's procedural statements from the SQL statements. For the pre-compiler to identify SQL statements, they must be marked. We do this by preceding them with **EXEC SQL**.

After pre-compilation, the program consists of two parts. One is modified source code which, besides procedural statements (here, "print" and "read"), consists of CALLs (of external routines) that replace the original SQL statements. We can handle this code just like any other code written in the host language. A standard compiler can translate it, producing an "object module", which can then be linked to the necessary libraries to form a "load module".

The other part consists of SQL commands. Depending on which database program one uses, it either compiles (binds) or analyzes (parses) the SQL statements. A compilation (SQL/DS and DB2) analyzes search strategies and then **creates** the machine code needed for an executable (access) module. An analysis (e.g., Oracle), finds the optimum search path, but creates the access module itself during execution.

The advantage of producing an executable module is that the optimal search paths need not be found every time the program is run. The disadvantage is apparent if you change the database. For example, suppose you delete a table or an index that the access strategy used. To form the optimum code, the access module must be **recompiled**. In the index case, recompilation occurs automatically, since there is no "error" but rather something missing.

Another problem arises if, for example, a new index is **created**. The access module will not record its existence, so an UPDATE STATISTICS must be performed occasionally. In this way, information that could be significant in optimization can form the basis of a recompilation of the access modules.

Parsing causes a search of the system directories to create access modules. The disadvantage, of course, is that this takes time (how much depends on the program code). We should note, however, that the system directories will either reside in RAM, or have their information stored redundantly (copied) so they are physically associated with the tables. In the latter case, not **all** directories but only ones related to individual tables must be examined. The advantage is that all changes are recorded so the access module formed at run time is always optimized.

Previous chapters have described SQL's "interactive" form (ISQL), in which the commands are executed in an interactive environment. Embedded SQL can use all of ISQL, but typically has other commands as well.

We now discuss the construction of an embedded SQL program and what happens when two types of programs must work together. There are minor variations in the order of handling individual parts that we will not treat here. We refer the reader instead to specific books and manuals.

9.2 DECLARE

The first statements in an embedded SQL program are declarations of the variables the host will encounter. The special problems here are ones that **both** the host and the database must use. We refer to them as "host variables". Their names may differ from the ones used in the tables. However, they must agree in type, and the rules for naming and type determination must follow the established rules of the host language. Variables used just in the procedural part (unrelated to database queries) must be declared in accordance with the rules of the host language and the pre-compiler.

The host variables are declared in a segment between the statements

```
EXEC SQL BEGIN DECLARE SECTION
```

and

```
EXEC SQL END DECLARE SECTION
```

The only things that may appear ahead of the declaration part are sequences that must come first in accordance with language rules. A typical example is the #include statements in C.

9.3 SQLCA

The next statement is

```
EXEC SQL INCLUDE SQLCA
```

SQLCA (SQL Communication Area) is a set of variables used by the DBMS and the host language to exchange information about the status of operations.

SQLCA itself is a variable of type **record** (struct in C). During execution, values are continuously written to its elements. One element is the numeric variable SQLCODE. It is a key part of SQLCA, as it governs the sequence of operations. The values assigned to SQLCODE during execution depend on which program one is using. The following **intervals** are generally accepted:

- Negative values indicate errors and make the program stop automatically. All changes are subject to a ROLLBACK. The text of the error that stopped execution appears in another element of SQLCA.

- Positive values are messages, indicating successful execution. There are only a few such values. 100 in SQL/DS and 1403 in Oracle are the most common, indicating that no record was found or that the search reached the end of the table.

- Zero means that everything executed correctly.

SQLCA is used internally during execution, but the programmer can and should use it to control program flow as well.

The pre-compiler creates SQLCA. Its construction and the names and types of its components are largely identical in all pre-compilers. The following is a typical example of a defined SQLCA (from SQL/DS 370/C):

```
struct sqlca
{
char                sqlcaid[8];
long                sqlcabc;
long                sqlcode;
short               sqlerrml;
unsigned char       sqlerrmc[70];
unsigned char       sqlerrp[8];
long                sqlerrd[8];
unsigned char       sqlwarn[11];
unsigned char       sqlext[5];
}
struct sqlca sqlca
#define SQLCODE    sqlca.sqlcode
```

Besides SQLCODE, SQLCA contains:

- The number of records affected by a DML command (an array element in sqlerrd).

- The text for SQLCODE (sqlerrmc).

- Information about disagreements between the lengths of host and table variables (an array element in sqlwarn).

- An indicator of whether NULL values occurred during the execution of a SELECT (sqlwarn).

9.4 The Actual Program

The program part (see Program 9-2 for an example) begins after the INCLUDE SQLCA statement. The first statement is often a logon procedure, which asks the user to enter an ID and a password. Then the actual program starts. It may begin with an ordinary SQL statement. More typically, it starts with an interactive dialog with the user, printing text on the screen and waiting for responses.

```
/* Example program to change an employee's salary */


EXEC SQL BEGIN DECLARE SECTION
    integer empno
    integer bpay
    integer withhold
EXEC SQL END DECLARE SECTION
```

```
EXEC SQL INCLUDE SQLCA

begin
print('Enter employee number:');read(empno)
print('Enter base salary:');read(bpay)
print('Enter withholding rate:');read(withhold)

EXEC SQL UPDATE employees
SET base_pay = :bpay, withholding = :withhold
WHERE employee_no = :empno
    print('employee', empno,' has a new base pay')
end
```

Program 9-2. Update an Employee Record

Program 9-2 first asks the user to enter an employee number, then it stores the value in the host variable empno. Next it asks for the employee's base pay and withholding tax rate. It stores their values in bpay and withhold, respectively.

After these preliminaries, the program changes the tables by executing SQL commands. A normal UPDATE command would be

```
UPDATE employees SET ...
```

but the embedded version requires an initial EXEC SQL to inform the pre-compiler that the statement requires special handling. When the program is executed, the host must pass data values to the DBMS. To indicate that the variables bpay, withhold, and empno require special treatment when used as variables in SQL statements, we precede them with a colon.

The last print statement uses empno, but just as an ordinary program variable. Thus it appears **without** the colon.

As mentioned, embedded SQL can insure entity integrity (the uniqueness of the primary key). For example, suppose we want to add a customer. Assume we have a unique index on customer_no which ensures that no two values are the same. How can the user find the next consecutive number? The solution is simple — just let the program find it. One approach (Program 9-3) requires a counter table. It has just two fields: "table_name" and "maximum". It contains a record for each table that has a primary key with consecutive values (customer_no, order_no, item_no, etc.). Each record has the table's name and the highest assigned key value. Part of the counter table might look like:

TABLE NAME	HIGHEST ASSIGNED VALUE
customers	1006
employees	56

Program 9-3 thus ensures that a new customer gets a unique number (customer_no).

```
EXEC SQL BEGIN DECLARE SECTION
   char cname[20]
   char sname[20]
   char city[20]
   number max
EXEC SQL END DECLARE SECTION

EXEC SQL INCLUDE SQLCA

/* Have user enter data */
print('Enter customer name:'); read(cname)
print('Enter street name:'); read(sname)
```

```
print('Enter city:'); read(city)

/* Get highest customer number from counter table */
EXEC SQL SELECT maximum
INTO :max
FROM counters
WHERE table_name = 'customers'
/* Insert data into record */
/* Customer number is highest value plus 1 */
EXEC SQL INSERT INTO customers
(customer_no, company_name, street_name, city)
VALUES(:max + 1, :cname, :sname, :city)

/* Update highest number in counter table */
EXEC SQL UPDATE counters
SET maximum = maximum + 1
WHERE table_name = 'customers'
```

Program 9-3. Find a New Primary Key Value

The counter table is not essential, as we could have

```
EXEC SQL SELECT MAX(customer_no) FROM customers...
```

instead of

```
EXEC SQL SELECT maximum INTO...
```

The advantage of the counter table is that only a single I/O operation is necessary to examine it. The alternative involves searching the entire customer table (requiring many I/O operations) to find the largest value of the primary key.

Program 9-3 shows two new aspects of embedded SQL, namely differences in the SELECT and INSERT statements. The change in INSERT is straightforward (it can perform computations on a value before storing it), but the changes in SELECT are more complex. All valid ISQL (Interactive SQL) statements are also valid in embedded SQL. However, SELECT typically returns a set of records, contrary to the procedural language's requirement of one record at a time. In the above example, the search fetches just one record (as there is only one that satisfies the condition). When this is true, we can use SELECT INTO to perform the search. If a SELECT returns multiple records, we need a new construct that can handle sets, namely a "cursor" (see Section 9.5).

The SQL commands mentioned so far all manipulate data. We can also embed DDL commands (such as CREATE TABLE or CREATE INDEX) or DCL commands. But note that we cannot use host variables in DDL statements, as they cannot be passed as parameters to them (see, however, **dynamic SQL**, as discussed in Section 9.8).

The following is thus illegal:

```
print('Enter name of new table:')
read(table_name)
EXEC SQL CREATE TABLE :table_name ...
```

The same holds for other DDL commands (such as ALTER or CREATE VIEW), since we cannot pass values (such as a table's name) to them using host variables.

There is, however, nothing wrong with executing complete DDL commands without parameters. Similarly, there is nothing to prevent the **creation** of a table (e.g., CREATE TABLE dummy) in embedded SQL, or the issuance of commands that **alter** a table structure. The only restriction is that one may not use variables, so the entire command must be written out. For example, the following SQL command is legal:

```
print('Index the customer table (y/n)? ')
read(answer)
if answer = 'y' then
EXEC SQL CREATE INDEX good_enough ON customers
   (customer_no)
endif
```

9.5 Cursors

When discussing SELECT, we limited ourselves to forms that return just one record. The reason is that SQL, as mentioned, operates on sets, whereas the host language operates on individual records. To remove the restriction, we need a mechanism that can fetch records from the set **one by one**. Such a mechanism is a **cursor**. The concept comes from video displays where a cursor indicates where the next character will appear. In other words, it indicates which part of the screen is active. A cursor in embedded SQL has a corresponding purpose, namely to indicate which record in a table is active. Its placement specifies a current record (often called, awkwardly, "current of cursor") that the program can access.

Before using a cursor, you must declare it with the command

```
EXEC SQL DECLARE cursor_name CURSOR FOR query
```

It declares a cursor with a name and an associated query (a SELECT statement), as in:

```
EXEC SQL DECLARE pointer1 CURSOR
FOR SELECT customer_no,company_name
FROM customers
```

There could, however, be cases involving both a SELECT and an UPDATE or a DELETE. The declaration of a cursor does **not** execute the associated query — it just specifies that the query exists. Only when the cursor is "opened" will the SELECT statement be executed.

To open the cursor "pointer1", enter the command

```
EXEC SQL OPEN pointer1
```

The cursor is placed **ahead** of the first record in the set derived using the SELECT statement. So it indicates the beginning of the chain that links the individual records in a table. The table is the active set that the cursor "points to". Nothing visible happens when the cursor is opened. You may compare the opening to tuning a radio dial to the far left (below the first actual station). It is also like opening a disk file.

The next step is a FETCH command that moves the cursor and provides access to a new record. For example,

```
EXEC SQL FETCH pointer1 INTO :customer_no,
    :company_name
```

moves the cursor to the first record in the active set. That record becomes the "current record". The cursor now "contains" data values. Still, nothing has occurred that is visible to the user. In the radio analogy, we have just moved the tuner to the leftmost (lowest numbered) station. The disk analogy is a SEEK command.

If the FETCH command is to work as intended, we must put it in a loop and associate it with a PRINT statement, as in:

```
WHILE true
EXEC SQL FETCH pointer1 INTO :customer_no,
    :company_name
PRINT(customer_no,company_name)
ENDWHILE
```

Now the cursor moves through the active set (the table). Each time it moves, we have a new "current record" for the PRINT command to reference. The cursor can only move forward, so there is no way to find the preceding record.

Eventually, the cursor will reach the end of the active set. You can recognize this condition by testing the integer value in SQLCODE of SQLCA after each movement. The default value is zero, indicating that an element in the set has been located. A special DBMS-dependent value indicates the last element, whereupon you can close the cursor with the command

```
EXEC SQL CLOSE pointer1
```

A closed cursor loses its active set and must be reopened before being used again. When a cursor is reopened, it positions itself at the first record, much like a typical disk file pointer.

For example, Program 9-4 lists employees in a particular department. It declares "personnel" to be a cursor for the department. The user then enters the department name and number, and the program opens the cursor and uses it to print a set of records. Note that we must declare the cursor, open it, and close it when we are done. The condition SQLCODE = 0 makes the loop continue as long as there are more records in the set.

```
/* List all employees in a department */
EXEC SQL BEGIN DECLARE SECTION
    int employee_no
    char department[3]
    char first_name[30]
    char last_name[30]
EXEC SQL END DECLARE SECTION
EXEC SQL INCLUDE SQLCA

BEGIN
    EXEC SQL DECLARE personnel CURSOR FOR
    SELECT employee_no,first_name,last_name
    FROM employees WHERE department = :department
    ORDER BY employee_no
print('Enter department code:')
read(department)


/* Here a check could test that the value entered
corresponds to an existing department. For example:

IF department < > 'A20' OR department < > 'A30' */

EXEC SQL OPEN personnel
print('In department: ',department,
    'are the following employees:')
WHILE SQLCODE = 0 DO
    FETCH personnel INTO
    :employee_no,:first_name,:last_name
    print(employee_no, first_name, last_name)
ENDWHILE
```

```
EXEC SQL CLOSE personnel
END
```

Program 9-4. Generating a Departmental Employee List

9.6 Using SQLCA

SQLCA is, as indicated, a communications area between SQL and the host language. It — or more precisely, a run time supervisor — is the agent that controls program execution. The value of SQLCODE determines how execution proceeds. If something goes wrong, it becomes negative, whereupon execution usually stops (depending on the program). All initiated but not COMMITted operations are canceled (an implicit ROLLBACK).

The applications programmer often wants to control the process. This is true both in program debugging and in handling user errors or warning messages. The run time supervisor's response to SQLCA is controlled by the statement

```
EXEC SQL WHENEVER error_type handling
```

The error_type can be SQLERROR, SQLWARNING, or NOT FOUND. It corresponds to the value of SQLCODE recorded in SQLCA. The exact value depends on the database program. The following features are, however, common to most implementations:

SQLERROR: SQLCODE is negative. An error has occurred that should cause execution to be suspended immediately.

NOT FOUND: SQLCODE is 100 (SQL/DS and DB2) or 1403 (Oracle). NOT FOUND is not an error message, but merely informs the user (or the program) that no record satisfied the query, or that the search reached the last record in the table.

SQLWARNING: SQLCODE has a positive value not equal to 100. SQLWARNING may be fatal and should be checked.

HANDLING describes what happens if one of the above SQLCODEs occurs during execution. It is thus the standard response to abnormal events (sometimes called *exception handling*). The alternatives are STOP, CONTINUE, or GO TO label. Their effects are as follows:

STOP terminates execution and does a ROLLBACK of all uncommitted transactions.

CONTINUE indicates that the program will proceed to subsequent instructions.

GOTO label causes the program to continue at the location specified by "label". It can, for example, force a jump to a subroutine that examines other elements of SQLCA (e.g., SQLERRMSG, which contains text describing the error). The subroutine can then report what it finds to the user. Depending on how serious the error is, the subroutine (see Program 9-5 for an example) may ROLLBACK the transaction.

```
/* Error handler using SQLCODE */
EXEC SQL WHENEVER SQLERROR
GOTO print_error_message
EXEC SQL WHENEVER NOT FOUND
GOTO print_error_message
```

```
EXEC SQL WHENEVER SQLWARNING
GOTO print_error_message

/* Update program goes here */
EXEC SQL COMMIT
print_error_message:
IF SQLCODE = 100 THEN
   PRINT('No records satisfy the query')
ELSE IF SQLCODE > 0 THEN
   PRINT SQLCA.SQLERRMSG /* Error message text */
ELSE IF SQLCODE < 0 THEN
   EXEC SQL ROLLBACK
   PRINT('A serious error has occurred ')
   PRINT('and no changes have been made.')
   PRINT('Update must be repeated...')
ENDIF
RETURN /* Return to caller */
```

Program 9-5. Error Handler Using SQLCODE

SQLCODE is particularly important in helping maintain database integrity. We mentioned the concept of a "transaction" when discussing integrity, and we will briefly repeat its definition here. A transaction is a logical unit (LUW or Logical Unit of Work), that may involve several **operations** or actions. An LUW consists of operations performed between two COMMIT commands or between a COMMIT and a ROLLBACK command (explicit or implicit). When a transaction ends with a COMMIT, the database is physically updated. That is, all changes made since the last COMMIT are made permanent in the database. The opposite, a ROLLBACK command, means that all such changes are removed from the database. Problems can arise in program execution if an LUW "breaks down" between two operations or while an update is being performed.

To avoid the consequences of an LUW not being completed properly, the statement

```
EXEC SQL WHENEVER SQLERROR GOTO error
```

can be useful. It can, for example, be used when implementing a cost of living pay increase for all employees. Suppose the program is updating the field base_pay. Since all employees, not just some, are to get a raise, we must complete the entire operation. We do not want an error to mean that some employees get the raise, whereas others do not. Imagine the difficulty of checking each employee record in a large organization to determine whether the base pay was adjusted properly. Those who did not get their increase would surely complain, whereas any who accidentally got it twice would not say a word!

Errors can also occur when an update involves several tables. For example, to maintain the integrity of the database when recording a sale, a transaction must change three tables as follows:

- It must create a new record (with order_no, customer_no, date, etc.) in the order table.

- It must create several new records (one for each item ordered) in the order_specs table. Each record must include order_no, item_no, and quantity.

- It must update (reduce) the quantity in the inventory table.

Program 9-6 shows how to ensure that all or none of the changes occur. Instead of using

```
EXEC SQL WHENEVER...
```

it tests SQLCODE directly. If an error occurs (SQLCODE becomes negative), it calls the function (procedure or subroutine) remove_the_change. A message that the programmer provides is passed via a parameter. The procedure (the declaration part is omitted) maintains integrity and prints the message.

The example appears to the end user as a single transaction, whereas three separate ones have actually occurred, together forming a logical unit. To put it another way, the transaction is accepted if and only if all three operations are performed correctly.

The reason why all three must be performed is to maintain consistency. For example, if the DBMS could not insert a record into the order_specs table, the company would end up with an order without products available. If the transaction continued, there would be fewer items in inventory **without** any actually having been sold.

The explicit test of SQLCODE means that if an error occurs during execution, the function remove_change is activated. It issues a ROLLBACK, which removes all changes, and sends the text in the variable "message" as a parameter to remove_change. In all other situations, all three partial transactions are COMMITted.

```
CHAR message[50]  /* Variable containing selectable
                     error text */


PRINT('Enter customer number'); READ(customer_no)
PRINT('Enter order number'); READ(order_no)


WHILE item_no <> 0 DO
   PRINT('Enter item no. and quantity or 0 to quit')
   READ(item_no,qty)
```

```
message = 'insertion in order table'
EXEC SQL INSERT INTO orders
   VALUES (:order_no, :customer_no)
IF SQLCODE < 0 THEN remove_change(message)


message = 'insertion in order_specs table'
EXEC SQL INSERT INTO order_specs
   VALUES (:order_no, :item_no, :qty)
IF SQLCODE < 0 THEN remove_change(message)


message = 'updating inventory'
EXEC SQL UPDATE inventory SET stock = stock - :qty
WHERE item_no = :item_no
IF SQLCODE < 0 THEN remove_change(message)
ENDWHILE


EXEC SQL COMMIT

remove_change(error_text)
PRINT('An error occurred during: ')
PRINT(error_text)
EXEC SQL ROLLBACK
```

Program 9-6. Updating Several Tables and Printing a Message via Parameter Passing

9.7 Indicator Variables

An indicator variable is a special type that is linked to a host variable both in the declaration part and in the program part. It indicates whether the linked host variable becomes NULL (i.e., takes on an unknown value) during a search. This is a problem in the host language, as it does not allow NULL values. When a NULL value is transferred to a host variable, SQLCODE becomes negative, and the program terminates. If indicator variables are used, the host variable remains unaltered (SQLCODE >= 0), whereas the indicator variable is assigned a negative value. Program 9-7 illustrates the use of indicator variables.

```
EXEC SQL BEGIN DECLARE SECTION
char h_first_name[20] :fn
char h_last_name[20] :ln
char h_department[3] :dept
EXEC SQL END DECLARE SECTION

EXEC SQL INCLUDE SQLCA
EXEC SQL DECLARE CURSOR pointer_2 FOR
EXEC SQL SELECT first_name,last_name,department
EXEC SQL OPEN pointer_2

WHILE SQLCODE <> 100 DO
   EXEC SQL FETCH pointer_2 INTO
   :h_first_name :fn, :h_last_name :ln, :h_department
   :dept
   PRINT(first_name, last_name, department)
   IF dept = -1 THEN
   PRINT('This person belongs to no department')
ENDWHILE
```

Program 9-7. Using Indicator Variables to Remove NULL Values
from the Host Variables

Note that the declaration part has indicator variables following the host variables. They are preceded by colons. Like other program variables, the indicator variables need not have a preceding colon when they serve standard functions in the host language.

Indicator variables can have the values:

-1 The table value placed in the host variable was NULL.

 0 The table variable was not NULL.

>0 The host variable was defined with too few elements. The table value was truncated.

9.8 Dynamic SQL

Dynamic SQL resembles embedded SQL. It also involves SQL statements within a host language program. The difference is that embedded SQL commands are compiled, whereas dynamic SQL ones are formulated by the end user **during execution**. From the program's point of view, the difference is that embedded SQL is compiled before execution, whereas dynamically declared SQL statements can only be compiled **when** executed. A key point is that the program does not know in advance how much space to reserve for variables, In practice, fewer end users will employ dynamic SQL than embedded SQL, as it requires extensive knowledge of SQL syntax.

EXECUTE IMMEDIATE

With the declaration part omitted, an ordinary embedded routine to increase an employee's base pay is:

```
print('Enter employee no.: )
read(emplno);
EXEC SQL UPDATE employees
SET base_pay = base_pay + 100
WHERE employee_no = :emplno
```

The embedded SQL command requires a fixed condition. What happens if the user knows only the employee's name or other characteristics? With dynamic SQL, the user can enter the condition, as in:

```
part1 = 'UPDATE employees '
part2 = 'SET base_pay = base_pay + 100 WHERE ';
print('Which employee is due a raise?');
print('Enter the condition: ');
read(part3);
strcat(part1,part2);
strcat(part1,part3);
EXEC SQL EXECUTE IMMEDIATE :part1
```

The routine works as follows:

- It sets the variables part1 and part2 (divided only to make the printed lines fit) to the string "UPDATE employees... WHERE".

- It asks the user to enter **the condition**. Typical examples are:

```
zip_code > '14000' AND zip_code < '14300'
base_pay BETWEEN 1300 AND 1500
```

- It saves the text of the condition in the variable part3.

- It uses the strcat (string concatenation) function to combine the command and the condition, saving the result in part1.

- It uses the EXECUTE IMMEDIATE command to compile and execute part1 at run time.

Dynamic SQL requires the user to understand both the data structure and SQL syntax. Otherwise, he or she cannot formulate the condition properly.

PREPARE - EXECUTE

EXECUTE IMMEDIATE does, however, have restrictions. The SQL command can neither perform a SELECT nor use host variables.

EXECUTE IMMEDIATE combines two sub-statements, namely:

```
EXEC SQL PREPARE
```

and

```
EXEC SQL EXECUTE
```

If we separate them, we can use host variables (but not SELECT). Another advantage of the PREPARE-EXECUTE sequence is that one PREPARE suffices for many executions.

For example, the following program segment gives different pay raises to different employees:

```
part1 = "UPDATE employees "
part2 = "SET base_pay = base_pay + :raise WHERE "
strcat(part1,part2);
while (raise <> 0) do
   print('Enter pay raise or 0 to quit:')
   read(raise)
   print('Enter condition:')
   read(part3)
   strcat(part1,part3);
   EXEC SQL PREPARE new_string FROM :part1;
   EXEC SQL EXECUTE new_string USING :raise;
endwhile
```

Note that "raise" serves as a host variable in the constant part2.

Dynamically Declared SELECTs

Neither EXECUTE IMMEDIATE nor PREPARE-EXECUTE can perform a query. But we can do one by declaring and opening a cursor, rather than using EXECUTE. The following is an example of a dynamically declared SELECT. It satisfies the restriction that the compiled program must know how many and which variables will be in the printout list before execution. The program first PREPAREs the dynamic statement. It then defines a cursor for it, just as though it were an ordinary embedded SQL statement.

```
part1 = 'SELECT first_name, last_name '
part2 = 'FROM employees WHERE '
print('Enter a condition: '); read(part3);
strcat(part1,part2);
```

```
strcat(part1,part3);
EXEC SQL PREPARE new_string FROM :part1;
EXEC SQL DECLARE pointer1 CURSOR FOR new_string
EXEC SQL OPEN pointer1;
while true do
    FETCH pointer1 INTO :host_first_name, :host_last_name
    print(host_first_name,host_last_name)
endwhile
```

The program must also know which variables are in the FETCH statement before execution. If one wants a dynamic printout list, the following problem can arise. The pre-compiler knows nothing about the numbers or types of host variables in the list. So storage space must be allocated during execution. The allocation is performed in the so-called SQL Descriptor Area (SQLDA), which — just like the SQLCA — must be included at the beginning of the program with the command

```
EXEC SQL INCLUDE SQLDA
```

SQLDA works with the DESCRIBE command. We will not treat its use further, as it is beyond the scope of our book.

9.9 Embedded SQL Example

Program 9-8 is a simple order entry system based on SQL commands embedded in C. For more information about the widely used C language, consult the following references:

Harbison, S.P. and G.L. Steele, Jr. *C:A Reference Manual*, 2nd ed. Englewood Cliffs, NJ: Prentice-Hall, 1987.

Kernighan, B.W. and D.M. Ritchie. *The C Programming Language*, 2nd ed. Englewood Cliffs, NJ: Prentice-Hall, 1988.

Swartz, R. *Doing Business with C*. Englewood Cliffs, NJ: Prentice-Hall, 1988.

```c
#include "stdio.h"
#define END_OF_TABLE 1403 /* SQLCODE for end of table */


EXEC SQL BEGIN DECLARE SECTION;
varchar user[25];
varchar code[25];
int counter;
int maxi;          /* Highest value */
int itemno;        /* Item number */
int emplno;        /* Employee number */
int custno;        /* Customer number */
int ordrno;        /* Order number */
int specno;        /* Number of items in order spec. */


char item[25];     /* Item */
char company[20];  /* Company name */
char street[20];


EXEC SQL END DECLARE SECTION;


EXEC SQL INCLUDE SQLCA;


/* Declare all functions */
void create( );
void data_entry( );
void error(char *);
```

```
void printout( );
void selection_menu( );
void terminate( );
void write( );


char *errortext;    /* Global variable with errortext */
main( )             /* Logon procedure */


{
printf("Enter your user ID: ");
scanf("%s",user.arr);
user.len = strlen(user.arr);


printf("Enter your password: ");
scanf("%s",code.arr);
code.len = strlen(code.arr);


EXEC SQL CONNECT :user IDENTIFIED BY :code;
EXEC SQL WHENEVER SQLERROR CONTINUE;


errortext = "logon procedure";
if(sqlca.sqlcode != 0) error(errortext);
/* If logon unsuccessful, report an error */


if(sqlca.sqlcode == 0) selection_menu( );
/* If logon succeeds, call selection_menu */
} /* End main */


void selection_menu( ) /* Select function from menu */
{
```

```
int choice;
system("cls"); /*   Call DOS command CLS (clear
                    screen) */
printf("\n\n\n\t\t");


printf ("CHOOSE AMONG THE FOLLOWING FUNCTIONS:");
printf("\n\n <1> Enter a new customer");
printf("\n <2> Print new order contents");
printf("\n <3> Data entry for new order");
printf("\n <0> Quit program");
printf("\n\n Please make a choice... ");
scanf("%d",&choice);
switch(choice)
   {
   case 0: EXEC SQL COMMIT WORK RELEASE;exit( );
   case 1: create( );break;
   case 2: printout( );break;
   case 3: data_entry( );break;
   }
}  /* End selection_menu */


void create( )    /* Function for creating a new
                     customer */
{


   errortext = "updating the counter table",
   /* Get highest customer number in use */
   EXEC SQL SELECT maximum
   INTO :counter
   FROM counters
   WHERE table_name = 'customers';
```

```
/* The table "counters" contains a record for each
table. It consists of just the table's name and the
highest primary key value assigned. This allows one to
quickly find the largest customer_no, order_no, etc.
without searching large tables. */


/* Get new customer number */
counter++;


/* Have user enter customer data */
printf("\n Enter company name: ");
gets(company);
printf("\n Enter street name: ");
gets(street);


errortext = "entry in customers table";


/* Put customer data in customer table */
EXEC SQL INSERT INTO
    customers(customer_no,company_name,street)
VALUES(:counter, :company, :street);


/* Update highest customer_no assigned */
EXEC SQL UPDATE COUNTERS
SET maximum = :counter
WHERE table_name = 'customers';
```

```
/* Commit new record */
EXEC SQL COMMIT WORK ;
printf("%s now created as number %d",company,counter);


/* End of customer record creation */
printf("\nPress any key when ready");
for(;;) if(kbhit( ) )    /* Wait for keypress */
selection_menu( );  /* Call main menu */


}
void printout( )
/* Function for printing customer orders */
{
printf("\n\n Enter a customer number: ");
scanf("%d",&custno);


errortext = "declaration of a cursor";


/* Declare cursor for customer orders */
EXEC SQL DECLARE pointer1 CURSOR FOR
SELECT order.order_no,item,order_specs.number
FROM order,order_specs,inventory
WHERE order.customer_no = :custno
AND order.order_no = order_specs.order_no
AND order_specs.item_no = inventory.item_no
ORDER BY order.order_no;


system("cls"); /* Clear screen */
errortext = "entry of orders";
```

```
/* Get company name */
EXEC SQL select company_name
INTO :company
FROM customers
WHERE customer_no = :custno;


printf("\n\n%s has the following orders: ",company);
printf("\n\t\tORDER NO \tITEM \t\t NUMBER \n ");


/* Print orders */
EXEC SQL OPEN pointer1;
for (;;)
    {
    EXEC SQL FETCH pointer1 INTO :ordrno,:item,:specno;


    if (sqlca.sqlcode < 0) error(errortext)
    else if (sqlca.sqlcode == END_OF_TABLE) terminate( );
    printf("\n\t\t%d \t\t%s \t%d",ordrno,item,specno);
    }
} /* end printout */


void terminate( )
{
EXEC SQL CLOSE pointer1;
printf("\nThere are no more records");
printf("\nPress any key when ready");
for(;;) if(kbhit( ))
selection_menu( );
}
```

```
void data_entry( )   /*   Function to enter data for an
                             order */
{


EXEC SQL WHENEVER SQLERROR CONTINUE;
char response;
system("cls");
/* Have user enter customer, employee numbers */
printf("\n Enter customer no.: ");scanf("%d",&custno);
printf(" Enter employee no.: ");scanf("%d",&emplno);
/* Determine next order number */
EXEC SQL SELECT maximum INTO :maxi
FROM counters WHERE table_name = 'orders';
maxi++;


EXEC SQL UPDATE counters
SET maximum = :maxi
WHERE table_name = 'orders';
errortext = "inserting record in order table";
EXEC SQL INSERT INTO orders
    (order_no,customer_no,employee_no)
    VALUES(:maxi,:custno,:emplno);
if (sqlca.sqlcode != 0) error(errortext);


response = 'Y';
   while (response != 'N')
   {
      /* Entry of order data */
      printf("\nEnter item no.: ");
      scanf("%d",&itemno);
      printf("Enter no. of items: ");
```

```
        scanf("%d",&specno);
        /* Records entered in order_specs table */
        errortext = "entry into order_specs table";


        EXEC SQL INSERT INTO
            order_specs(order_no,itemno,number)
        VALUES (:maxi, :itemno, :specno);
        if (sqlca.sqlcode != 0) error(errortext);


        /* Inventory updated */
        errortext = "updating inventory";


        EXEC SQL UPDATE inventory
        SET number = number - :specno
        WHERE item_no = :itemno;
        if (sqlca.sqlcode != 0) error(errortext);


        printf("\nEnter more data (Y/N)?");
        response = tolower(getche( ));


        switch (response)
            {
            case 'n': write( );break;
            case 'y': continue;
            }
    } /* End while */
} /* End data_entry */


void write( )   /* Function that commits entered data */
    {
    printf("\nChanges are written to the database");
```

```
        EXEC SQL COMMIT WORK;
        printf(" ... done");
        printf("\n\nPress any key when ready!");
        for(;;) if(kbhit( ));
     selection_menu( );
     }  /* End write */


void error(char *text) /* Function which:
     prints errortext (transferred by parameter)
     prints sqlcode (sqlca.sqlcode)
     prints official errortext (sqlca.sqlerrm.sqlerrmc)
     performs a rollback */
     {


     printf("\An error has occurred at %s",text);
     printf("\nPLEASE REPORT THE FOLLOWING TO YOUR DBA");
     printf("\nsqlcode error: %d",sqlca.sqlcode);
     printf("\nwhich means: %s",sqlca.sqlerrm.sqlerrmc);
     printf("\n\n No changes made");
     EXEC SQL ROLLBACK WORK ;
     printf("\n\nPress any key when ready!");
     for(;;) if (kbhit( ));
     selection_menu( );
     } /* End error */
```

Program 9-8. Order Entry System Using SQL Embedded in C

10

Applications

We have noted previously that SQL is not user-friendly. It presumes users know a great deal about the language's syntax, as well as the structure and meaning of the underlying database. Thus there is an obvious need for methods and packages (or applications) that make SQL easier to use. Such packages often provide ways to specify operations using either forms (as in query by example) or menus.

Chapter 9 described an approach that involves combining SQL statements with an ordinary programming language (embedded SQL). Its major advantage is that host language routines can handle all data manipulation (entry, updating, and deletion). Furthermore, such routines can enforce database integrity and provide validity checks on data entries, computation of sequential elements, and interactive user interfaces. Dynamic SQL offers even more flexibility and user control. It also allows for the implementation of all data definition tasks (creating and altering structures) as routines.

This chapter covers two alternatives to embedded SQL, namely OS/2's Database Manager and Oracle's SQL*Forms. We do not directly compare them, as they have different purposes and audiences. OS/2's Database Manager provides user access to all of SQL, whereas SQL*Forms is strictly a screen generator. For completeness, we should note that SQL/DS also has a screen generator called QMF (Query Management Facility).

10.1 OS/2 Database Manager (Database Services)

As shown in Figure 10-1, the OS/2 Database Manager consists of three parts (like Caesar's Gaul). (SQL) Database Services forms the basis for working with databases under OS/2. It corresponds to SQL/DS, which we discussed previously, under MVS. A Query Manager (QM) and an Application Program Interface (API) are supplements to Database Services. They allow for database access methods such as embedded SQL.

```
┌─────────────────────┬─────────────────────┐
│       Query         │    Application      │
│      Manager        │      Program        │
│       (QM)          │  Interface (API)    │
├─────────────────────┴─────────────────────┤
│         SQL Database Services              │
└───────────────────────────────────────────┘
```

Figure 10-1. Model of the OS/2 Database Manager.

We should note that OS/2 Extended Edition requires a powerful IBM PS/2 or compatible with at least 20 MB of disk space and 3 MB of RAM available for its own use. Furthermore, OS/2 provides many ways to extract data from a database and export it to a concurrent program such as a spreadsheet, word processor or desktop publisher, or graphics program. For more details on OS/2. see R. Borland, *Running OS/2* (Redmond, WA: Microsoft Press, 1991) and R. Duncan, *Advanced OS/2 Programming* (Redmond, WA: Microsoft Press, 1990).

If you examine OS/2's list of "future reserved words", you can see that there are plans to expand the SQL dialect significantly. For example, PRIMARY KEY, FOREIGN KEY, DELETE, and CASCADE are all reserved. The idea is surely to add many functions corresponding to ones already in mainframe SQL/DS, thus promoting a continuity of applications on different platforms (as specified in IBM's Systems Application Architecture or SAA). There are also new functions such as "procedures" and procedural elements (CASE, ELSE, and WHEN). OS/2 also can work like a small mainframe operating system, thus allowing SQL to work in a distributed or network configuration. A prerequisite is, however, a LAN server (see the *Microsoft System Journal* issues of July and November 1988).

We will discuss only the Query Manager here, as it provides an alternative way for a user to operate on a database with SQL. In fact, we cover only limited aspects of QM, namely its report, menu, and procedure facilities. For more details on other aspects of the OS/2 Database Manager, see H. Fosdick, *OS/2 Database Manager: A Developer's Guide* (New York: Wiley, 1989).

The SQL dialect used with Query Manager is the ANSI standard. There is nothing special about it except that the user does not know he or she is dealing with SQL. In short, one need never see or write an actual SQL statement when working with QM. One may **choose** to do so, but it is not required. The new feature of QM is the shell it creates around the database and its tables containing, among other things:

- menus for data definition (DDL)

- menus for data manipulation (DML), including the creation of views and indexes

- report writing procedures and facilities

- panels (screen displays) that can show several tables and their connections

- facilities for creating user menus

In practice, not everyone likes menu-driven systems, mice, and fixed, predefined choices. Experienced professionals often find them slow and confining. If you want, you can leave the friendly environment and use SQL directly by writing commands. You can also switch between the two environments. Obviously, such facilities are only for the chosen few, and most users (particularly occasional ones) would surely prefer the shell to "naked" SQL.

We should note the importance of the function keys when using QM, as they often provide shortcuts. All options are **also** available via combinations of function keys and the Alt, Ctrl, and Shift keys. So you need not always choose from a menu; you can execute a function directly even though it is not currently displayed. We call the direct method a "hot key" or "speed key".

Query Manager

When Database Manager is active, and the employee, customer, and order tables described previously in this book have been created, the opening screen display will appear as shown in Figure 10-2 (slightly edited). Note the menu bar at the top, the availability of help (via

F1), and the list of databases (called a **pick list**) at the bottom. The >
sign indicates the current position of the cursor (the actual indicator
is system-dependent).

```
Actions    Tools    System    Exit        F1 = Help

                        Databases

     Select a name and press F10

     Name             Comment

     ■  —NEW—          Open a new database
     >  EMPLOYEES
     ■  CUSTOMERS
     ■  ORDERS
```

Figure 10-2. Typical opening screen display in Query Manager.

If you now select the employee table by pointing to it (with the
mouse) and then select Actions from the menu bar, the display
summarized in Figure 10-3 appears. Note that the menu bar, title,
directions, and pick list have all changed to reflect the new situation.
F1 still activates help, as indicated in the top right corner. The actual
screen also contains descriptions of what the selections mean.

```
┌──────────────────────────────────────────────┬───────────────┐
│ Commands              Exit                     │ F1 = Help     │
├──────────────────────────────────────────────┴───────────────┤
│                                                                │
│               Main selection for EMPLOYEES                     │
│                                                                │
│    Select an item; then press Enter                            │
│                                                                │
│    ■  1. Tables and views                                      │
│    >  2. Queries                                               │
│    ■  3. Forms                                                 │
│    ■  4. Procedures                                            │
│    ■  5. Panels                                                │
│    ■  6. Menus                                                 │
│    ■  7. Profiles                                              │
│                                                                │
└────────────────────────────────────────────────────────────────┘
```

Figure 10-3. Actions menu in Query Manager.

Unlike SQL*Forms (described later), QM is a product for both end users and applications programmers. Selection 4 from the Actions menu (Procedures) is used to prepare programs (in a language resembling VM/SP's REXX). The programs can be ordinary routines, and can also call predefined panels. Panels are screen displays formed using selection 5 and can involve either a freely selected or a standard format. An individual panel (consisting of one or more screens) can contain the printout of data from various tables. Panels can also define connections between tables so that, for example, a particular customer's name and vital information always appears along with his or her orders.

Selection 6 (Menus) lets you define menus from which an end user can make selections. A selection from a user-defined menu can cause the execution of a procedure. You can thus create a menu-driven interface without special programming.

So far, the features we have described are unrelated to SQL. They are typical of a wide range of menu-driven application builders.

Selections 1 and 2 in Figure 10-3 provide QM's SQL interface. Selection 1 (Tables and views) has the options shown in Figure 10-4.

```
Actions      Commands      Tools      Exit   │   F1 = Help
─────────────────────────────────────────────────────────────
  ■  1. Open definition
  >  2. Add data rows
  ■  3. Change data rows
  ■  4. Change ID for list
  ■  5. Erase
  ■  6. Add index
  ■  7. Show index
  ■  8. Erase index
─────────────────────────────────────────────────────────────
  Esc = Cancel
```

Figure 10-4. Menu for working with tables and views.

For example, if the user chooses selection 1 (corresponding to DDL commands), a new screen appears. Its first choice determines whether we are defining a table or a view. For a table, the user must enter the column names, types (here he or she can enter the type manually or choose among the possible ones), lengths, and attributes (NULL or NOT NULL). After completing this part, the user must name the table, and the definition is then saved.

The user can now proceed to other menu options (Figure 10-4), namely insertion, update, deletion, or index operations. At no point in the process does the user have to remember SQL syntax rules, field names, or table names. The user can always get a listing of available options, and point to a command and execute it by pressing the mouse buttons a few times.

Queries (selection 2 in Figure 10-3) are executed similarly. However, there are two other options. One is to repeat a previously defined and named search. This resembles the batch file or macro capability of many operating systems and other packages, or the search commands of popular word processors. The other is to choose commands from the menu in Figure 10-4 and write a query using standard SQL syntax. You can then name and save it. Of course, this approach is only suitable for those knowledgeable in SQL.

The third possibility is, as with creating tables, to use the mouse. To prepare a query this way (called **prompted queries**), you must first specify the tables involved. You can obtain a list of all table names and just point to the ones you want searched. Next a new menu appears from which you can select columns to be printed. Then you must prepare the query itself by making choices. First, you select the field to be used, the verb (IS or IS NOT), and a comparison operator (equal to, less than, greater than, etc.). Afterward you must choose which columns are to be compared, and so on. The reason for the method's name should now be evident.

The advantage of the menu-driven approach is that users can write SQL commands without knowing any syntax. The disadvantage is equally obvious - it takes a long time to make all the choices. But, as we mentioned earlier, you can write your own commands, use the function keys, or choose a combination of the three methods. The alternatives clearly allow for a wide range of preferences, backgrounds, and experience levels.

10.2 SQL*Forms

Many facilities mentioned in the discussion of OS/2's Database Manager are also in Oracle's popular collection of tools: SQL*Calc (a spreadsheet), SQL*Plus (an SQL implementation), SQL*Forms (a screen generator), SQL*Report (a report generator), and PRO*xxx (an interface to C, FORTRAN, and COBOL, among other languages). SQL*CASE (Computer Aided System Engineering) is also available for system developers.

We will describe only SQL*Forms, and it just briefly. (Note parenthetically that Oracle can run under OS/2, and under MS-DOS on a PC/AT or PS/2. It requires an Intel 80286 CPU, plus at least 1.5 MB of extended RAM and 15 MB of disk space).

Unlike OS/2's Database Manager, which allows users both to define and create tables and to manipulate their data without knowing SQL, SQL*Forms is a tool for the applications programmer. Only the results are made available to the end user.

SQL*Forms also differs from OS/2's Database Manager in that it is intended only for manipulating tables, not for creating them. On the other hand, the available options, particularly in the area of relating tables, are a significant advance over SQL. With the aid of SQL*Forms, a database no longer appears as a helter-skelter collection of individual tables but rather as a tightly integrated structure of related data.

SQL*Forms is an independent application activated from the operating system. The term "form" here means a set of related screen displays. After you create a form, you must "compile" it. Later you can activate it from the operating system, another application program, or other forms. The applications programmer works with SQL*Forms itself (creating forms) via popup menus.

The first thing you must do upon entering SQL*Forms is name the form you want to create. A named form consists of named "blocks". A block in turn, consists of fields that refer to a base table (or view), come from other blocks, or serve exclusively as data entry fields. A block is not like a window but rather is a named sequence of connected fields.

Besides the screen display itself (the form), SQL*Forms provides two key elements for use in defining blocks and fields. One is a trigger, comparable to a procedure in a programming language. Triggers may be activated when the user, for example, moves into or out of fields, changes a field, deletes or inserts a record, or moves to another block. The other feature is that you can specify the properties of a field, for example, whether it **must** have a value, whether its value must lie in a specified range, or whether it may be updated. Furthermore, forms are accessible only to end users who can identify themselves with a user ID and password.

Blocks

A form consists of blocks. So creating a form requires defining blocks and their characteristics. There are two ways to define a block. You can specify it either as a standard (default) block or as a "free block".

A standard block is associated with a particular base table or view. So it may include any (or all) fields from the table. But it may include other fields as well. Typical examples are fields from other blocks or "virtual fields", the values of which are computed from other fields.

Unlike a default block, you must build a "free block" from the ground up. That is, you must define all of its fields. They can come from a database table. A block that is not associated with a particular table must be created as a "free block". The lack of association with a table is the only difference between it and a default block.

Note the following about the block in Figure 10-5. It consists of just one unit named "customer_data". We form it as a "default block", i.e., it includes all fields from the base table (customers). Its fields have the same names as the table's fields.

```
Customer no.:              Type:
Company name:              Telephone:


Street:
Zip Code:
```

Figure 10-5. Modified standard (default) block.

The city is missing from the block, as it is part of another table (zip_codes). We can link it to the block as a non-table element. The important fact to note here is not that we can do this, but that we can do it using a trigger.

Triggers

A trigger is a procedure executed when a particular event occurs. The event could be an update or an insertion. Many types of triggers exist (including Roy Rogers' famous horse), so we will mention only a few examples here. A trigger can, for example, execute on any of the following conditions:

- Before the cursor moves into a field ("pre-field" trigger) or when it leaves ("post-field" trigger).

- Before the cursor moves into a block ("pre-block" trigger) or when it leaves ("post-block" trigger).

- Before or after a record is deleted ("pre-delete" or "post-delete" trigger).

- Before or after a change in the field tables ("pre-update" or "post-update" trigger).

- After a change of the field value in the block ("post-change" trigger).

- When a particular function key is pressed.

- After another trigger executes.

The user can thus define triggers and let them execute as part of other triggers or be activated by function keys. By specifying triggers to be activated, we can redefine all the function keys. Triggers thus resemble the popular terminate-and-stay resident (TSR), keyboard macro, or popup utility routines available in many systems. A trigger may contain most legal SQL commands, as well as ones specific to SQL*Forms.

For example, suppose we want to include the city name (from the Zip Code table) in the customer data block (Figure 10-5). We must create a field for it and associate it with the Zip Code. We connect the two fields via the following post-change trigger in the zip_code block field:

```
SELECT city
INTO :customer_data.city
FROM zip_codes
WHERE customer_data.zip_code = zip_code
```

To distinguish screen data from table data, we prefix screen field names with a colon.

After the form is compiled and the user activates it, the post-change trigger works as follows. When the user enters the Zip Code and leaves the field, it fetches the city name automatically from the Zip Code table and places it in the field :customer_data.city. Thus, the Zip Code and the city name always correspond, ensuring the referential integrity of the database. We have eliminated the possibility of a user entering the wrong city name, obtaining an incorrect Zip Code, or making a typing or spelling error.

Data Manipulation

The user does all data manipulation via the function keys. That is, there are function keys for INSERT, DELETE, UPDATE, and SELECT. The most important one selects the records to be handled, since, in contrast to SQL, one can only manipulate data on the screen. An update involves first finding the relevant records. When the data values in a record appear in the corresponding block fields, the user must move the cursor to the specified field and enter the new value.

Similarly, to delete a record, you must first find it. Once it is found, you can delete it by pressing a function key. To create new records, you press a function key to clear the screen and make room for the new values.

There are several ways to search for particular records. When you have a form on the screen, the simplest way to search is by pressing the appropriate function key. The screen clears, and you can fill the fields to be used in the search with values. Then the search can be executed. We refer to the approach as **query by example** (QBE). Its advantage is that the user need not know SQL syntax to search a table.

If you enter values in several fields, the search condition is the logical AND of all of them. For example, the two entries in Figure 10-6 are translated into the SQL statement:

```
SELECT customer_no,type,company_name,telephone,
    street,zip_code
FROM customers
WHERE type = 'C' AND zip_code > '12400'
```

```
Customer no.:              Type: C
Company name:              Telephone:

Street:
Zip Code: > 12400          City:
```

Figure 10-6. Using query by example to search a single table.

By using the function keys for "fetch previous record" and "fetch next record", you can move back and forth through the records that satisfy the search criteria. The limitations here are that you can only search a single table and can only use the logical operator AND.

You can do more complex searches, but they require knowledge of SQL. If you enter a symbol in a field and then press the "query" function key, the following message appears at the bottom of the screen: "Query where?:". You can then enter a condition as you would in SQL. It could, for example, be:

```
Query where?: zip_code > '14000'
```

However, the restriction to searching a single table still applies.

A final search option involves having a trigger exit to the SQL command prompt by suspending form work temporarily. Once at the prompt, you can search as usual — without, however, affecting the form with which you are currently working.

Working with Several Tables

A form may contain data from many tables. Figure 10-4 refers to just one table, and the user sees just one record at a time. One characteristic of a block is the way in which data is presented. You can specify that more than one record from the table should appear. For example, suppose we create a default block for the order table (block_name=order_data), and specify that up to five records (at a time) from it may be displayed. Figure 10-7 shows the screen for "customer_no=1003".

There is no advantage here unless we can connect the customer data and the order data. The connection can, as mentioned, involve a trigger, but you can also define the field :order_data.customer_no as a **copy** of the contents of the customer number field of the previous block (:customer_data.customer_no).

```
Customer no: 1003                Telephone: 2324354
Company: Lehigh High School  Type: S


Street: 76 Farm Street
Zip code: 14031                  City: Clarence
```

Customer_no	Employee_no	Shipped
1003	22	16-AUG-89
1003	22	17-AUG-89
1003	22	30-AUG-89

Figure 10-7. Displaying data from several tables and several records from a table.

When you are making queries on the customer_data block (the customer table), you can provide several triggers that act on other blocks. We mention only one of them here, namely a **KEY-NXTREC** trigger (a so called "macro trigger"):

```
#EXEMACRO NXTREC; NXTBLK; EXEQRY;
 GOBLK CUSTOMER_DATA;
```

The result is that if one presses the next record (NXTREC) function key, the macro does the following:

1. Fetches the next record (NXTREC = NeXt RECord) into the customer_data block.

   This fills in all the fields, including the Zip Code. Because zip_code has a post-change trigger, the city name is automatically fetched and placed in the city field.

2.   Goes to the next block (NXTBLK = NeXT BLocK), i.e., order_data. The field customer_no has, of course, been set to customer_no from the previous block (customer_data).

3.   Executes the query (EXEQRY = EXEcute QueRY), and fetches five records (or as many as exist) from the order table into the block.

4.   Returns the cursor to the customer_data block.

A field can have many triggers. In the above example, we could have PRVREC (PReVious RECord) and EXEQRY (EXEcute QueRY) triggers with the same contents as the NXTREC trigger. We could initiate them when users want to examine the previous record or after they perform a query, respectively.

The limitation that one can only search a single table still applies. However, as the copied field here is a join predicate, the above search (together with the defined triggers) is equivalent to the following two searches undertaken as one:

```
SELECT customer_no, type, company_name,
    telephone, street, zip_code
FROM customers
WHERE type = 'C' AND zip_code > '12400'
```

and

```
SELECT customer_no, employee_no, received,
    shipped
FROM orders
WHERE customer_no = :customer_data.customer_no
    (previous block)
```

Integrity

We can thus use triggers to connect tables or blocks and assure that the data represents the relationships in the original design. We can also define connections and triggers to help maintain database integrity. Another use for triggers is in generating new, unique identification numbers. For example, to get a new customer number, we could create a pre-insert trigger (for the block) that automatically fetches the largest value for customer_no (from the customer table) and then uses it plus 1 in the new record. We could also specify the field as not user-alterable, so users cannot change the sequence.

Triggers can also validate data entries. One could do a range check, i.e., determine whether an entry lies in a specified interval. If we delete a record from the customer table, a pre-delete trigger could, for example, check whether there are corresponding records in the order table. If so, it could delete them, transfer unshipped orders to another table, or do something else. It might, for example, pass the data to a C program activated from the form.

Domains

We defined a **domain** previously as the set of permissible values for an attribute. SQL*Forms does not support domains directly. However, if we regard them as tables (for example, the inventory table contains the set of valid item names), there are several ways to implement them. If, for example, we enter a new record into the order_specs table, we can do domain checking by creating a pre-insert trigger that searches the inventory table to see whether the item exists. It can then commit the entry if the domain check succeeds.

The best approach to domain checking depends on the number of possible values (the size of the domain). The question here is not programming difficulty, but rather practical matters of efficiency.

If the domain has just a few elements (for example, the entries in the employee table), one can have them appear when the user presses a particular function key. The user can then page through them and select one. To ensure only valid entries, we can specify the field as "non-updatable". The user cannot enter data into it directly. Thus the use of domains contributes to integrity, as the user can only select among acceptable values. Of course, we know only that the entry is valid, not that it is correct.

If the number of possible values is large (as with item names), you can create a new form that displays them. For example, we could have a trigger activate it when the user moves the cursor into the field. We can define the new form to prevent the user from changing the data values. All he or she can do is search through them and point to the desired value. The trigger then copies the data via global variables back to the original form.

Triggers can do much more. For example, a trigger can be the equivalent of a CASE structure in a traditional programming language. With it, you can create menus from which the user can select, as shown below. Note that Oracle has a built-in utility, SQL*Menu, for this task.

```
Choose among the following entries:

New customer:            1
New order:               2
New employee:            3


Enter choice:__
```

You can define a CASE MACRO on the choice field as follows:

```
#EXEMACRO CASE CHOICE IS
WHEN '1' THEN CALL CUSTOMERS;
WHEN '2' THEN CALL ORDERS;
WHEN '3' THEN CALL EMPLOYEES;
END CASE;
```

Here CUSTOMERS, ORDERS, and EMPLOYEES refer to forms that perform the desired operations. When combined with a startup macro automatically initiated when Oracle is called, the CASE option provides an excellent user interface.

11

Architecture

So far, we have said little about how the DBMS finds data. This chapter describes briefly the formal structure of a database, the implementation of physical and logical independence, and the agents that define and manipulate data.

Figure 11-1 is a simplified model of database architecture. It shows the database as composed of physical and logical levels, here separated by a dashed line. The DBMS controls the logical level, and the computer's OS controls the physical level. Do not think of the dashed line as a hardware/software boundary, since current systems may implement the file manager partly in hardware (via a database machine) and disk drivers may depend on disk controller hardware that is an entire computer in its own right.

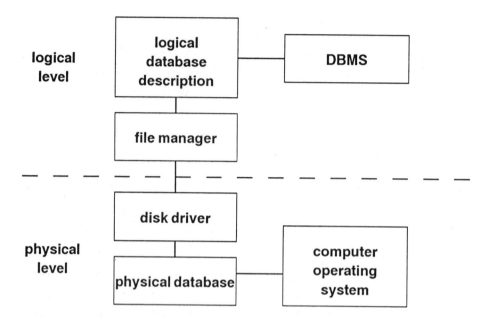

Figure 11-1. Overall database architecture.

11.1 Data Independence

There are many **reasons** for separating the logical and physical levels. For example, it allows the DBA to alter the storage format or media without changing the database (the logical organization) itself. Physical data independence also allows the DBA to do the following:

- Cluster tables. Remember that clustering (see Chapter 5) means that data that logically belongs together (such as customer_no and company_name from the customer table, and orders the customer has placed) lie close together physically.

- Create or remove indexes.

- Store old data sequentially in a separate table on a magnetic tape or other backup medium. It can thus be archived to save disk space and reduce costs, while still retaining historical audit records.

- Pack data using a compression method.

- Upgrade system hardware (CPU, memory, and peripherals) or software. This is essential in a period of rapid technological change. Ten year old equipment is often hopelessly obsolete, expensive or impossible to maintain, and an object of ridicule from staff and users alike. New versions of major software packages (including operating systems) arrive every few years, often with important new features or corrections that make their installation essential. Software packages also may become obsolete, fall out of use, or lose their support.

If a database program supports physical data independence, the DBA can implement these changes without having to make more than minor revisions to the logical structure and the applications. The reason is the existence of an address mapping between the logical and physical levels. The available options depend, of course, on which database software one is using.

Note that relational database theory says little about the physical level. The two products used in our examples support physical data independence in the sense that you can reorganize physical databases. With SQL/DS, the reorganization depends on facilities in specific IBM operating systems. Oracle, on the other hand, is completely independent of the hardware selected and thus also of the operating system chosen. It runs on a wide variety of computers and under many different OSs.

Because relational database systems are independent of the physical environment, they are well suited for implementing **distributed** databases, as the DBMS does not need to know how and where the data is actually stored. Particularly if we are dealing with **heterogeneous** systems involving a variety of different hardware and software, physical data independence is essential. Oracle, for example, can run on all machines in a distributed or networked environment, including supercomputers, mainframes, mini- computers, workstations, and PCs.

A prerequisite for supporting physical data independence is the existence of a third level, namely a communicating agent (acting like a network manager) that translates (via mappings) between the logical and physical levels. The agent has two major components. One is a file manager at the logical level that operates on tabular data organized in "dataspaces". We can regard a dataspace as a large address space in which each record has an address. The other component is a disk driver at the physical level that translates between dataspace addresses and physical addresses in a storage medium.

The next step is to also require "logical data independence". The idea here is to create more levels at which we can have different environments. For example, we must provide database security entirely at the logical level. Often many users with varied needs and privilege levels must work with a database. Logical data independence lets us establish and maintain a security model without affecting either the logical or physical levels. The security aspects operate only at the logical level, deciding who has what access to which data at a specific time. Each class or type of secure user has its own environment. Similar models could exist for privacy or other features.

Another advantage of logical data independence is that large administrative units often require many different operating environments. Departments such as accounting, finance, personnel, marketing, engineering, research and development, sales, public relations, manufacturing, and maintenance all have different needs, requiring different logical structures for the same overall database. Even within departments, groups frequently have special needs. New issues also arise, particularly in today's fast changing business and government worlds.

A database is logically data independent if queries (directly from SQL or from programs) do not depend on its overall logical structure. For example, the DBA may want to split the employee table into two tables recording, respectively, base data and salary data. Using the relational approach, we could implement logical data independence by preparing a view (called "employees") as a join of the two new tables. The result is that all applications that previously operated on the employee base table would now use the employee view instead.

The establishment of standards for multi-level database systems began in the early 1970s. The CODASYL group, an outgrowth of the group that defined the COBOL language, distinguished three levels in a logical database. The ANSI/SPARC group later extended and expanded the CODASYL group's work. The basic model remained the same, namely a three-level description. In ANSI/SPARC terminology, the levels are the "external schema", "conceptual schema", and "internal schema". The word "schema" has roughly the same meaning as "definition", but it sounds more mysterious and is therefore technically preferable. We may describe the three levels as follows.

The **external schema** is the part of the database with which the user has direct contact. It typically consist of subsets of the overall database. In relational databases, it corresponds to **views** based on the entire database. The user can access the subsets via a high level language such as SQL, an application, or a combination. We define the access method in Chapter 4 as consisting of a host language plus a data sublanguage.

The **conceptual schema** is a definition of the total database, i.e., all tables, security measures, view definitions, and so on. The DBMS controls the mapping between the levels and the user's access via a language. The system catalog supports the mapping.

The **internal schema** describes how data is stored, what format it has, and which indexes are available. A file manager represents it here. This agent (a program) considers the stored data (tables) as occupying a logical address space without regard to the underlying physical files.

The three levels are most clearly distinguished in network databases where one can define them and the mappings with commands such as

```
SCHEMA NAME IS schema_name...
STORAGE SCHEMA NAME IS storage_name...
```

and

```
MAPPING FOR...
```

Relational databases omit the MAPPING FOR command deliberately to assure physical independence. The DBMS itself must create and maintain the mappings.

The **physical database** is maintained separately from and outside the database architecture. A discussion of it must deal with subjects such as tracks, cylinders, sectors, blocks, bytes, and bits. The computer's OS controls the physical database via the disk driver (the I/O software in the operating system that works with the file manager). For a detailed example of a typical disk driver and file manager, see A.S. Tanenbaum, *Operating Systems: Design and Implementation* (Englewood Cliffs, NJ: Prentice-Hall, 1987).

The separation between physical and logical levels is particularly important in the theory of relational databases. The reason is that one declared goal of the theory is independence of the physical environment. So it cannot say anything about physical conditions. Of course, the database program must contain information that allows for communication across the border.

11.2 Logical Database

Before describing the logical database, we should note that the implementations of databases (both logical and physical) are system dependent. There are differences, for example, that depend on whether the hardware is a PC or PS/2 (as with the PC version of Oracle) or a mainframe (as with SQL/DS). The structures do not differ greatly due to the emphasis on independence of the physical level. However, there are differences in terminology and in the logical to physical interface. The following discussion is general and notes significant differences in implementations.

The box in Figure 11-1 marked "logical database description" contains all information necessary for the DBMS to operate. The system catalog contains all required information about tables, indexes, views, access modules (programs or compiled SQL statements), security features, and so on.

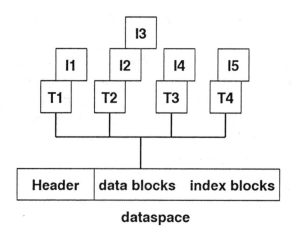

Figure 11-2. Organization of tables and indexes into logical dataspaces.

Figure 11-2 shows four tables (T1 through T4) and five associated indexes (I1 through I5). The figure also indicates that the tables and indexes are all part of a dataspace. The header at the beginning of the dataspace contains general information about its organization.

According to the model, the data is stored in a dataspace. But this is true only from the DBMS's point of view. A dataspace is a logical way of organizing data in an infinite linear address space. The model does not account for which files are used, whether several tables share a file, or whether the files are spread among several physical disks. The DBMS thus regards a database as simply consisting of a collection of tables and records. On receiving a query, the DBMS consults the system catalog and interprets it (acting as a command interpreter) in accordance with this perception.

One side of the dataspace thus faces up toward the DBMS. The other side faces down toward the disk driver and the physical database. A dataspace corresponds in the relational model to the internal schema of the ANSI/SPARC description and uses the file manager in Figure 11-1 as the implementing agent. Note that a file is a logical element, the **name** of a particular location on a physical disk.

A dataspace may be divided into many subordinate dataspaces. The file manager and disk driver handle translations between the logical dataspace and the physical address space (volumes, cylinders, tracks, sectors, and pages or blocks). The driver, as its name suggests, actually handles the details of disk operations. It finds the physical pages or blocks that the file manager uses.

We must define a dataspace before creating tables, because each table must have an associated logical address space. In SQL/DS, we create a space using the command

```
ADD PUBLIC DBSPACE
```

or

```
ADD PRIVATE DBSPACE
```

It must be followed by

```
ACQUIRE PUBLIC DBSPACE space_name
```

or

```
ACQUIRE PRIVATE DBSPACE space_name
```

In Oracle, we create a space with the rather obvious command

```
CREATE SPACE space_name
```

We define a dataspace with parameters that, among other things, specify its maximum size (in blocks), how many blocks are reserved for indexes, and how much space per block is reserved for updates. Remember that the dataspace is a logical description. All parameters refer to an as yet unfilled physical address space.

Of course, we can compute how large dataspaces must be to contain our tables. We simply estimate how many records of what size each table could require. The dataspace should typically be twice as large as the estimate. There is no advantage to making it small, as it does not use any physical storage space **before** we associate data with it. All we are defining is the number and addresses of blocks that it could occupy. In SQL/DS, for example, the definition of a dbspace of 128 empty blocks requires a single KB. An oversized dataspace is no catastrophe, whereas one that is too small can cause problems when we must move data from it to a larger dataspace. In SQL/DS, we must select a size carefully because we cannot change it later.

Oracle, on the other hand, allows changes in all parameters of the space definition. You can expand both the logical address space (the number of dataspaces) and the physical storage while working with the database. Expanding physical storage is a matter of increasing the number of **files** (in Oracle's PC version) or DBEXTENTS (disks) in SQL/DS used to store data.

All tables and indexes must be associated with a dataspace. We make the connection when we create a table structure. The user can explicitly tell the system to place a table in a particular dataspace with the command

```
CREATE TABLE customers
 (customer_no INTEGER,
   .

   .    )
IN SPACE customer_space
```

If the IN SPACE clause is not present, the system assigns the table to a default dataspace.

The advantages of controlling the placement of tables are system specific, but they depend on how we treat the data. For example, it is often advantageous to assign each large table to its own dataspace, so sequential searches through it need not skip over the data of other tables (thus minimizing I/O operations). SQL/DS also allows you to store data in "private" or "public" dataspaces, making it accessible only by some users or by everyone.

A further logical organization involves associating minidisks (or Oracle files) in logical units called "storage pools" (IBM) or "partitions" (Oracle). The advantage (only in SQL/DS) is that we can specifically define the pools as "non-recoverable" (the default is "recoverable"). The system then need not store and log changes in the table data. Data can only go in a non-recoverable storage pool if it never changes.

Of course, multiple dataspaces have disadvantages as well. Extra I/O operations are often necessary when joining tables.

11.3 Physical Database

If we read Figure 11-1 from the bottom up, it shows that the physical database is the foundation of all data handling. Physical data is stored on the disk bit by bit. The bits are organized in "flat" physical files identified by names. Each file has a unique starting and ending address (disk number, cylinder number, track number, or similar designation). To work with a file, one can simply let the operating system's disk driver find it. On-line databases, however, require more organization, as many tables can be in the same large file. One needs, therefore, more direct access to particular parts of files. The subunits one uses are "blocks" or "pages", physical areas of the storage medium. They are uniquely identifiable within, for example, a track. The block size is typically a few KB.

We can thus interpret the model specifically as follows. Before we create the first table, a dataspace exists (due to the space definition) of, e.g., 256 logical blocks numbered from 0 to 255. Each block has a physical address (for example, cylinder number, track number, and sector number).

Once we define a dataspace, we can create tables in it and associate them with it. A dataspace consists of many blocks. Viewed from the file manager's side, they form a logical **page set** that initially contains only the (addresses of) empty blocks. We refer to this page set as the *empty page set*.

11.4 Logical-Physical Interface

The following discussion assumes no tables and thus no data in the database. Furthermore, we assume, for simplicity, that a physical block can contain only a single record.

Creating a table structure (with CREATE TABLE) does not affect the dataspaces with which one works, since the DBMS has its own dataspaces for information about tables and their definitions. Thus, without further complications, we can create the customer table.

When we put the first record in the table, the DBMS will receive an inquiry about it from SQL. The DBMS interprets the inquiry as concerning tables. It does not know how data is stored or recorded. It can only save **records** in a table structure, so it asks the file manager to do the job. The file manager now does two things. First, it associates the record with dataspace address 1 (the first address in the space). Second, it must get the disk driver to find room for the record. It therefore asks the driver to locate the first block in the empty page set and to release it as data storage for the customer table.

The actions create a new page set (the empty one already exists), which the page manager associates with the customer table. The new page set is uniquely identified via an ID, but we will simply call it the customer page set.

After the new page set is created, data storage can begin. The driver places the data (the first record) in the first block (block 1, as block 0 is reserved for special use). If there is more data, it will go in subsequent blocks. In this case, however, we enter only one record.

Next we create the order table. When we enter its first record, the DBMS once again asks the file manager to find room in the space. Thus it creates yet another page set, called "orders". The file manager asks the disk driver to use the first available block of the empty page set for data about orders. So it goes in block 2.

Suppose we enter more customer records. The disk driver fetches another block from the empty set. This time it is used for the customer page set. At this point, the occupied part of the disk might appear as shown in Figure 11-3.

No 1	Previous 0 Next 3	No 2	Previous 0 Next 5	No 3	Previous 1 Next 12
1002 East Side Club 65 High St. 14250 339-8070		2001 1002 33 03-AUG-89 15-AUG-89		1001 South Ball Club 1 Club St. 14031 327-5432	
Unused space		Unused space		Unused space	

Figure 11-3. Appearance of physical disk blocks after record entry.

The block numbers are in the top left corner. The header also holds the addresses of the next and previous blocks containing data from the same page set (i.e., **logically** associated data). Block 1 (customer data) thus is linked to block 3, which also contains customer data. Block 3, in turn, is linked to block 12. The disk driver can use the pointer structure to read data from a particular page set.

The addresses of chained blocks may also be in the header. They are used, for example, when a table contains a field defined as a VARCHAR. A VARCHAR is actually stored in a block (perhaps in another format) elsewhere on the disk. The header contains only a pointer to it.

The next three rows are the data block itself. The example would be more realistic if each block had data from many records, perhaps even from different tables.

The file manager must handle the blocks. It will try, of course, to save as much data as possible in them. Only when there is no more room will it ask the disk driver for new blocks. However, it will never split a record between two blocks unless the table is defined with an initial value greater than the block size. A CHAR value, for example, defined as CHAR(30), but which contains only the string "nets", will be stored as four bytes (plus overhead for the current length and location within the block). If we now update the field so it contains "tennis nets", the file manager will find room in the block by using the segment marked "Unused space" in the figure. How much such space each block contains is a parameter (PCTFREE) in the space definition.

Only UPDATE (not INSERT) uses the segment reserved for "Unused space". After all, new records (created by INSERT) are placed in blocks fetched from the empty page set. Thus INSERT does not cause a physical reorganization of existing data. The reservation also affects indexes associated with a table. An index is, of course, a specification of the physical addresses of individual records via a RecordID (RID). The availability of space for updates means that the system seldom must change the RIDs of individual records. If the blocks had no buffer, an insertion (or removal) of records would require a time consuming updating of the index. When records are deleted, empty areas occur in the blocks, and the data becomes "fragmented". To avoid excessive fragmentation and wasted space, the system must occasionally reorganize the data physically. The process is time-consuming and typically involves moving many records.

A more realistic situation is one in which pages can contain data from several records. Here the data entry order determines the contents of the individual blocks. With only some records entered, one could have a block organized as shown in Figure 11-4.

Now the file manager needs more information, namely **where** in each block individual records begin. The system uses this to localize logically associated data (also necessary if blocks contain data from several tables). The address is computed by specifying an offset such as the number of bytes from the start of the block to the beginning of the record. The block number and the offset (the location of the record within the block) form the record's RecordID, or simply RID.

Some programs allow users access to RIDs. In practice, this seldom makes sense because the RID changes when you insert or delete records or when internal reorganization occurs.

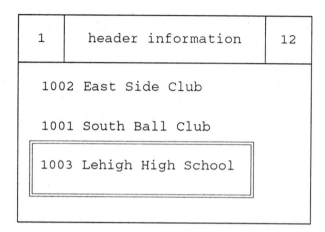

Figure 11-4. Single block with data from several records.

Using a page set associated with a particular table and the RIDs, the file manager can uniquely identify all records in a dataspace. The manager uses the information, for example, to determine where to store updated records. We should note that the disk driver, of course, knows nothing about the data values in the blocks. A query such as

```
SELECT company_name FROM customers WHERE
zip_code = '14031'
```

is not something it can handle. Whether the individual records from the customers dataspace satisfy the search criteria is up to the DBMS to decide after the driver fetched the records into RAM.

The disk driver does the following jobs:

- Takes blocks from the empty set and assigns them to a named page set. When an entire block is emptied, the driver must return it to the empty set.

- **Searches for** and reads blocks the file manager requests via **commands such as:**

```
Fetch the first block in the orders page set
Fetch the next block in the orders page set
```

- Maintains the mapping between blocks in a page set and their physical locations.

To perform such tasks, the disk driver needs to know where page sets **begin** in the physical address space. The mapping of page set names into base addresses is often located in block 0, the header block as shown in Figure 11-5.

```
No | Previous
0  | Next
   |
customers       block  1
orders          block  2
employees       block 18
zip_code        block 22
order_specs     block 12
inventory       block  7
```

Figure 11-5. Header block with starting addresses of individual page sets.

Only rarely will block 0 alone contain this information. Often systems reserve the first few blocks.

Consider the following SQL command as an example.

```
SELECT *
FROM customers, orders
WHERE customers.customer_no = orders.customer_no
AND customers.customer_no = 1002
```

To perform the query (specified via standard or embedded SQL), the DBMS must do the following:

- Check the syntax.

- Use the system catalog to verify the existence of the specified tables and columns.

- Determine whether the user is authorized to perform the query.

- Evaluate the query to decide whether it should search through customers first and then orders or vice versa, i.e., optimize the search.

- Determine whether an index exists on the tables. If one does, the procedure differs (see Section 11.5).

- Inform the file manager which tables are involved.

Thus the DBMS does not work with the actual data at all, but only with table **definitions**. It views data as possibly existing stored records.

The file manager must now do the following:

- Identify the dataspace containing the tables.

- Tell the disk driver which page sets contain the required records (both customers and orders).

- Let the disk driver do the rest of the work, i.e., find the physical addresses at the beginning of the various page sets and then follow the pointers in the block headers.

The file manager regards data (the individual tables) as a page set. But it cannot simply fetch the records the DBMS wants. What the file manager can do - working with the disk driver - is identify the required logical blocks (in the dataspace), and then let the driver decide whether to fetch the entire block (i.e., the file manager serves as an I/O operator). When the file manager gets the block, it must "translate" its contents into a form the DBMS can understand, namely a record with a structure corresponding to what appears in the system catalog. Note that the driver fetches the entire **block** into RAM (or buffers).

After the block has been fetched into RAM, the DBMS takes over again. Its task is to read sequentially through the available records. In the example, the DBMS optimizes the search by first dealing with the customer table, as it contains only one relevant record. After the records from the order table are fetched, the DBMS can select ones with "customer_no=1002" and then perform the required joins and printouts.

11.5 Reorganization

When several tables share disk space, logically connected data will end up being dispersed over a large area. This is a typical result of executing many INSERT and DELETE commands. The blocks that form a page set will no longer be physically continuous. We should also note that the disk driver itself insures that empty blocks (ones emptied by a DELETE) are automatically transferred to the empty space. But this occurs only for completely empty blocks. Partially empty ones are left alone. The end result is extra disk I/O operations to skip over empty or unrelated blocks when examining data from a table.

The DBA can judge how fragmented the data is by examining the system catalog and other statistics, such as the number of I/O operations. There are two ways to reduce fragmentation. One applies after the fact, and the other is preventive.

After determining that the data is fragmented, the DBA must "re-allocate" it, i.e., change its placement. He or she can do this by first saving the data in a temporary table (or just an ordinary file), then removing the fragmented table from the page set. This takes time, of course, if it involves reorganizing just one table from a dataspace, as the file manager must move many addresses around and the disk driver must move a lot of data to fill the now available blocks. But once it is done, the DBA can move the table back into the dataspace, thus assuring that data that logically belongs together now also is physically close together. To save overall time, one often prefers to simply copy the entire dataspace, empty or remove it, and then restore the data.

The preventive method involves assigning each table to a separate dataspace. This avoids mixing data from different tables, but, as indicated, also means more I/O activity when joining tables from different spaces.

11.6 Indexes

When defining a dataspace, one specifies how much of it is to hold data blocks and how much index blocks. The percentages one chooses depend, of course, on the anticipated activity, but typically we reserve between 20% and 30% of the total dataspace for index blocks.

Control over how much room is reserved for index blocks involves the parameters CREATE SPACE (Oracle) or ACQUIRE DBSPACE (SQL/DS). The two systems differ in that SQL/DS requires advance specification of the percentage dedicated to indexes. The blocks cannot be used for anything else, and they cannot be changed by an ALTER DBSPACE command. In Oracle, three parameters specify the initial reservation of space, the step in blocks by which it may be expanded, and, finally, how many times it can be expanded.

To show how indexes work, consider the following command:

```
SELECT * FROM inventory WHERE item_no = 4093
```

If we first assume neither indexes nor clusters, the file manager must perform a sequential search of the disk. In other words, it must find the first entry in the page set containing the inventory table and transfer its identification to the disk driver. The disk driver must now find the block address and search for the first block belonging to the space holding the inventory table. Then the file manager must locate the next entry in the inventory page set that the driver must fetch (possibly after having moved the read/write head), then the next, etc.

The process changes if logically connected blocks are physically connected via a pointer structure (as in Figure 11-3). Then further work can be done without the file manager intervening. The process continues until a record is found in which "item_no=4093". But even then the sequential search must proceed, since the DBMS does not know whether the record is unique. The search therefore continues until it finds an empty pointer to the next logical block. The result is a large amount of I/O activity.

The idea behind indexing is simply to bypass the file manager, as the DBMS now knows more about the address mapping between records and physical blocks. All the file manager must do in indexed searches is report where (in which blocks) the index is physically stored. If a unique index exists on the primary key, the DBMS will discover it upon examining the system catalog. It then knows that there can be at most one record that satisfies the search criterion. Chapter 5 noted that an index is an ordered list (or a B-tree, another type of list). So even though there are, for example, 100 identical data values in the index, they will always be located in RAM simultaneously. Only if the indexed data value plus the pointer (the address) occupies more than one block will extra I/O occur.

When an index (B^+-tree) is created, the sequential part (see Chapter 5) contains a pointer for each element. What we use here is the unique identification of where a particular record is: the block number. The block number is thus the pointer in the index. The result is a slightly different procedure. First the index must be loaded into RAM (if it is not already there). The file manager does this by asking the disk driver to fetch it.

Once the index is in RAM, the DBMS can search down through the tree and quickly find the address of the record it wants. The DBMS can now transfer the address directly to the disk driver and ask it to fetch precisely the block containing the desired record. If the index is in RAM, only one operation is required; otherwise, two are necessary. Of course, the index may be too large for a single block, so that several blocks must be copied from disk to RAM. This does not, however, greatly increase the number of time consuming I/O operations, since the index blocks are physically contiguous and fetching them involves, therefore, some read/write head movement but little extra access time.

If the index is not unique (e.g., customer_no in the order table), there will, of course, be more searches and more disk I/O. However, there will still be fewer overall I/O operations, because the individual blocks can be fetched immediately and an indexed search ends at the last index entry, **not** at the last page in the set.

11.7 Clusters

We discussed clusters in Chapter 5 as a method of changing the physical placement of data on the disk. Its effect is to reduce the number of I/O operations required by some searches.

If, for example, we cluster the customer and order tables, the disk would appear as shown in Figure 11-6 (the dates are omitted).

No 1	Previous 0 Next 3	No 2	Previous 1 Next 3	No 3	Previous 1 Next 0	No 4	P
	1002 East Side Club 65 High St 14250 339-8070		2001 33 2008 56 2016 56		2018 56 2019 33		1003 Lehi 1403
	Unused space		Unused space		Unused space		

Figure 11-6. Blocks with data organized as a cluster.

If a cluster structure is created, block 0 (the directory block) must be expanded to contain information about which tables are involved. The header information must also be expanded for the primary table so that a query can follow another pointer chain.

Note also how redundant information disappears because the order table is superimposed on the customer table. Customer_no **would** have been redundant, but the clustering removes it. The major disadvantage is also obvious — there is no longer any direct access to the order table. A search such as

```
SELECT * FROM orders WHERE customer_no = 1002
```

must be done via the customer table. Note that we can still create an index or perform searches based on customer number in the order table. The DBMS merely interprets the commands differently.

The above discussion is greatly simplified. Among other things, the order data in block 2 clearly belongs to customer 1002, because its page set also must be able to be accessed as an independent data set. Also block 4 must follow block 3 if all data in the cluster must be used.

Besides removing redundant information, clustering also reduces I/O operations in common searches involving the customer and order tables (in that order). If we also create a (cluster) index on the customer table (customer_no), the individual blocks containing customer data can be fetched directly via it. Thus we can also reach the orders associated with the customer.

Figure 11-6 shows an interfile cluster, in which the main table occupies a block by itself. The situation is unrealistic, as a block usually contains data from both the main table and the ones associated with it.

We can also form intrafile clusters, each involving a single table. This has two advantages. First, data that logically belongs together is also often searched for at the same time. This is true, for example, of the order table if a particular customer's orders are often printed together. In that case, it would be advantageous to cluster on customer_no. Storing a table (e.g., the order_specs table) as an intrafile cluster has little advantage (except for removing redundant information). The data will, of course, generally be entered at one time, so that logically related data is already close together physically.

The other advantage of this storage method is that many records have data in common. An American survey indicated, for example, that of 1.2 million **different** last names, just 1500 constitute half of them. A similar pattern holds for telephone numbers, which can be clustered around area codes. The idea of clustering is partly to provide rapid searching for connected records, and partly to reduce redundant information around the cluster column. Finally, an option is often available for compressing data.

Since clustering changes the physical location of data (the storage method), it also has disadvantages. Among other things, it will certainly spread out other connected data and thus reduce the speed of other searches.

12

Configurations

Many varied applications use databases. Airlines, hotels, and car rental agencies have reservation systems; government agencies, corporations, and nonprofit institutions have personnel management, payroll, and accounting systems; banks, insurance companies, stockbrokers, and mutual funds have account management systems; and supermarkets, department stores, and specialty store chains have centralized inventory. The list goes on. In most retail transactions, the customer can pay with an authorized check or credit card. In other words, most daily business activities now involve some kind of database operation. Of course, differences exist. The fast food restaurant where the counterperson presses a key to sell a cholesterol-laden hamburger does not need a mainframe. The database inside the cash register is sufficient to determine the exorbitant price. On the other hand, banks need large computers to track their wise investments in junk bonds, overvalued real estate, and third world debt.

Currently, many different database systems exist. They vary greatly in size, power, cost, expandibility, flexibility, and orientation toward particular environments and applications. This chapter briefly examines today's most common and most promising architectures.

In ancient times when dinosaurs (mostly from IBM) ruled the world, there were no PCs, and mainframe solutions were inflexible, expensive, and difficult to develop and manage. Today, most mainframes are part of a total data processing (or information management) solution involving minicomputers, workstations, PCs, networks, and even supercomputers. Small machines, linked by local area networks, handle an ever-increasing share of the computing workload.

We can distinguish two broad categories of computing systems: single-user and multiuser. Whereas most single-user systems are very much alike, we can further classify multiuser systems into three basic configurations: centralized, decentralized, and distributed.

Using our sports equipment firm example as a basis (reading about it is almost as good for you as actual exercise!), this chapter examines the advantages and disadvantages of different configurations. We emphasize distributed systems, as they are rapidly increasing in numbers and importance.

12.1 Single-User Systems

The simplest configuration is the single-user system (Figure 12-1). In databases, we can regard it as representing "the good old days" when men were men, right was might, and everything was still "easy to understand": one user, one database, one CPU, one storage location, etc. Most PCs (and PC-based databases) still use this configuration. So it is far and away the most common environment, as there are today millions of stand-alone PCs, not connected to networks, mainframes, or anything else.

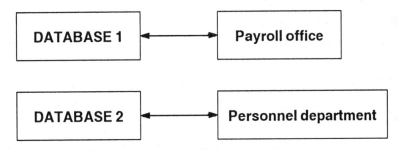

Figure 12-1. Typical single-user system.

Obviously, single-user systems offer tremendous advantages, or they would not have proliferated so rapidly. In the first place, system components are close together, so communications is highly reliable and very fast. There is no dependence on telephone lines or other links. No time is spent on buffering, formatting, or other overhead activities.

The single-user system need not coordinate its activities with anything. It need not spend time worrying about locks, deadlock, or other such problems. Furthermore, the system does not depend on the correct operation of, or availability of, outside resources such as a central computer, network server, communications channel, or operations staff.

However, single-user systems do have disadvantages. One is limited processing power. Even the most powerful PC or workstation cannot match a large mainframe for solving big problems. Many practical database problems involve complex calculations or huge amounts of data.

A database-specific issue is the difficulty of maintaining the integrity of information spread over many machines. For example, in Figure 12-1 both databases must contain information about employees. So some data (name, address, etc.) must be stored redundantly. To preserve referential integrity, we would have to update this data by making changes in both places. Consider as an example an employee who is promoted, moves, or is fired. We must change information in two physically independent databases. Obviously, the probability of errors and inconsistencies depends directly on the number of databases and increases rapidly as it rises.

Another weakness of the single-user configuration is that every user must provide for backup, security, privacy, and other key features. Also, applications often must be present in many machines, thus requiring the purchase, maintenance, and upgrading of software in several places.

Many disadvantages of single-user systems disappear in multi-user systems (both "centralized" and "hierarchical" configurations). In larger organizations, multiuser systems dominate because of the need to access centralized databases, maintain security and integrity, and handle large amounts of data.

12.2 Centralized Multiuser Systems

Figure 12-2 shows a configuration centered around a mainframe that services many terminals. The terminals have no local processing power (that is, they lack user CPUs, so they are called "dumb terminals"). Other variants are possible. We could have a LAN (Local Area Network) with a server connected to many PCs, or we could use PCs instead of terminals. One possibility is to have the server CPU handle all database operations, while the PCs function both as terminals and as local processors. With software on individual PCs to emulate a terminal and transfer files, users can fetch data from the database, put it in PC files, and process it further using the PC's own text editor, statistical or graphics package, or spreadsheet. After the downloading, data is typically no longer in the form of tables but rather in standard data files. The option also exists of copying the data to a PC DBMS and processing it as tables. Of course, this works best with products such as Oracle that run in many different environments.

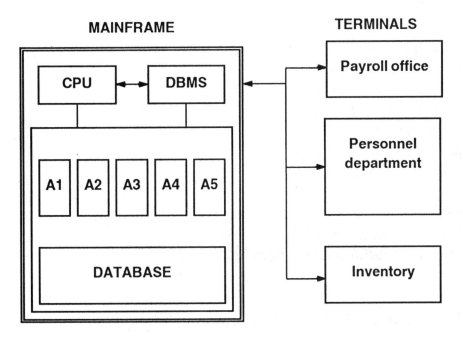

Figure 12-2. Typical centralized configuration.

In Figure 12-2, A1 through A5 are database applications programs. They may either be commercial products, such as report generators, graphics tools, or form generators (for creating screen images), or custom programs specifically designed for a particular database function. There may be routines for consistency control, safeguarding of referential integrity, improved communications between user and machine, error handling, security management, and data analysis.

Centralized configurations often have communications problems. The response rate for user terminals depends on the speed and reliability of the communications lines. They may be expensive and may introduce a large amount of overhead. In a typical configuration, a central computer communicates with remote terminals over the public telephone system or a private data network. The remote user is dependent on the performance and availability of both the central computer and the communications system.

In practice, centralized systems require central management. An independent computing department (or information center) is necessary, as is a DBA. The department is responsible for constructing and maintaining the database and for managing the tools and services that make it usable. In particular, the central department must handle the following tasks.

Design: Information center personnel can do all logical and physical design work. They can specify all data definitions and manipulations and handle the creation, updating, and maintenance of the physical storage structure.

Integrity: Since the database is centralized, integrity only has to be maintained and secured in one place, i.e., in the central computer. However, note the problem of users downloading data, then maintaining it in their own machines. Such data may be obsolete or inconsistent.

Archiving: The central management can handle all backup, auditing, and log tasks. Only the information center has to be concerned with salvaging damaged files.

Security: The information center can provide security against unauthorized use of the database through user identification or authentication, passwords, and the auditing of improper actions. Note, however, that data downloaded to user terminals may not be secure.

Optimization: Using special performance analysis tools, the DBA can keep informed about the database's operation. He or she can recognize and replace inappropriate routines and hardware. The DBA can also determine where bottlenecks are occurring and plan for future enhancements, changes, or additions.

Applications: The advantage of having all applications on the main computer is that everyone can use them, thus saving storage capacity. Another benefit is that maintenance and upgrading of applications and database software only has to occur on one computer.

Much of the work done by end users involves custom applications, often based on or combined with purchased software. Examples are routines for entering new customers, updating inventory, tracking or analyzing orders, etc. Routines may also exist to check data consistency or perform other validation tasks. These applications only have to be maintained and updated in one place.

Maintenance: Only the information center needs the expertise required to keep the system working. That is, local groups need not have DBAs, systems operators, or applications programmers.

The major disadvantage of a centralized solution is that the failure of a strategically significant element affects everyone. If worst comes to worst, a central failure may affect the vital functions of the organization. Less spectacularly, high-priority work (such as executive paychecks) or maintenance operations may make the entire system temporarily and unpredictably unavailable.

The centralization of processing power, data, and applications can lead to other problems as well. Some examples are:

- Each change in a terminal's screen image, whether caused by the user typing or the computer reporting results, requires data transmission. Although individual alphanumeric terminals have small needs (2KB per screen), they do add up. Modern bit-mapped graphics terminals with more advanced and friendlier user interfaces exacerbate the problem. For example, a workstation with 1024 x 1024 graphics in 256 colors requires 1MB per screen. Obviously, the trend is toward greater use of graphics terminals for design work, desktop publishing, and other applications.

- Many users need access to the same data and programs. So the CPU must manage the resources, giving jobs priorities either through a democratic "round robin" solution or some other method. It must serve different users in turn and must, therefore, spend time scheduling, moving data and programs between disk and memory (swapping or paging), resuming interrupted work, etc. Overhead can increase rapidly, bogging down the system.

- A user waiting to enter new data for a specific order (in the order_specs table) must assume that a lock (exclusive or shared update) has been put on the inventory table. Meanwhile, others cannot use the locked table. So the DBMS must maintain lock tables and avoid or resolve deadlocks. The granularity of locks is important (i.e., how much data must be locked for a transaction to be performed).

- A user wanting to make a query through an application on, say, the order table, but not wanting to update it, must presuppose a shared lock on the table. Other users must not update it during the operation.

In multiuser systems, one can never completely escape the problem of some users having to wait for a table or other resource to be released. Whether this causes poor response times depends on the choice of hardware, systems and database software, and logical database design. We can improve the situation by upgrading the hardware, for example, by adding a controller that has enough memory capacity and intelligence to generate screen images for several terminals.

12.3 Decentralized Configurations

The decentralized configuration solves some problems mentioned above. It consists of units that can work independently. Such a configuration may involve each department having its own mainframe as shown in Figure 12-3. The mainframes may have many terminals attached (not shown in the figure).

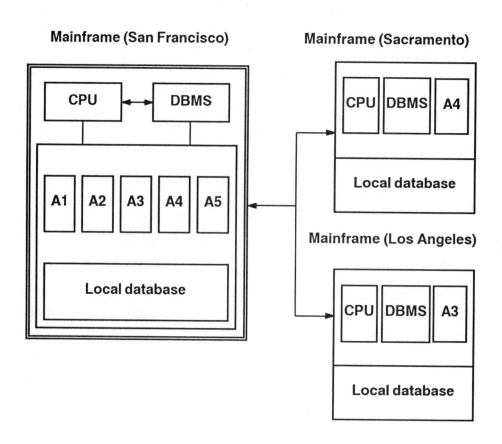

Figure 12.3. Typical decentralized configuration.

The decentralized configuration has both data and applications located where they are needed. It may consist of independent units, each of which itself is centralized, but which can exchange data files. Such exchanges are generally uncommon and may be both slow and relatively difficult to implement. The end result is that data on one unit is not readily available to the others (as it is in the distributed configuration discussed later).

The decentralized configuration often involves a large central database that is updated only occasionally. A typical situation would be a bank with individual branches that function mainly as independent units during working hours. Using local databases during the day is faster and more convenient because they are smaller. Errors are localized, and the single central update (at night) allows time for extensive validation and reduces the chances of accidental corruption.

Returning to the sports equipment company, decentralization allows a customer in San Francisco to order items from the branch in Sacramento. During the day, both units keep separate records for the customer. After hours, the system transfers all transactions to the central machine that stores and maintains all orders. Note that the integrity of the database is questionable during the day, and many clever criminal schemes have taken advantage of temporary lapses.[1] This configuration also implies that the system transfers data belonging to individual departments from the central machine to the local computers every morning.

The characteristic of decentralized systems is that data is not a common resource. Users must specifically request files from other machines and must explicitly transfer them. They cannot casually search or operate on data stored elsewhere. To reduce the number of slow transfers, decentralized systems often have the same data (such as inventory records) stored redundantly in several places. An unfortunate consequence is loss of consistency. The individual department cannot be sure that the screen display is correct because another department may have sold the items.

---

1   Parker, D.B. *Computer Crime: Criminal Justice Resource Manual*, Washington, D.C: National Institute of Justice, 1989.

12.4 Distributed Configurations

The last configuration we treat decentralizes the data. We refer to it as a "distributed" system because data is spread out over different and often geographically separated machines. In contrast to the decentralized configuration, data is a common resource, meaning that all users can work with any of it.

Also, applications are distributed, so they need not be present in all local units. In general, local operations must have some information management expertise, but as data is the common property of all machines, everything can in principle be controlled from one place.

The concept behind distributed systems is to put data and applications where they are used. The idea is to minimize expensive, slow communications, while still maintaining the availability, consistency, and integrity of the databases. We refer to the geographically separate machines as "sites" or "nodes".

Definition

When describing database architecture (Chapter 11), we divided the definition into three levels (external, conceptual, and internal schema). The distributed solution requires two more levels, a "global schema" and an "allocations schema". In between, there is a "fragment schema" that defines the connection (mapping) between them (Figure 12-4). Remember, a schema is basically just a definition.

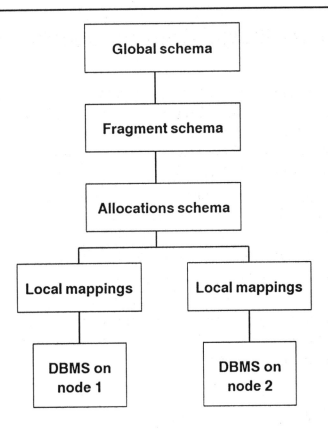

Figure 12-4. Typical distributed architecture.

The global schema defines the overall database. In the relational context, it consists of all data available for use in all nodes. It is organized as tables. The global schema defines the database without regard to its physical distribution. It consists of tables that can be divided into any number of subsets or "fragments" stored in different places. The fragment schema defines the division into subsets.

The allocations schema defines the physical allocations of individual fragments. It also indicates whether they are stored redundantly. An example of redundant storage would be to keep the Zip Code table in all local machines to reduce the need for communications. This makes sense as the table seldom requires updating.

When a redundantly stored table does require updating, we must be sure that changes occur everywhere. The fragment schema contains the required information.

From the two new schemas comes the definition of the local databases (local DBMSs). In the system implementation, individual machines have their own data that they can manipulate locally. They also know where the other data in the global schema is located. We often use the term "transparency" to describe the situation, referring specifically to location transparency, fragmentation transparency, etc.

Transparency is a requirement for physical and logical data independence. The distributed system must operate as though it were not distributed at all, and the user must be able to work on the database without considering the distribution or even knowing that it exists.

Implementation

Some DBMS's permit the definition of several databases on the same or different machines and also allow work to be performed on several databases. We do not regard the result as a distributed system, since users cannot work on several machines and several databases "simultaneously". They must terminate work on one database and begin work on another. The prerequisite for having a distributed database is that the user can connect to another database ("awaken" it) and make it do a task (such as fetching data) "at the same time" as the first one is running, and, for example, join tables from the two.

In the following, we assume that data is distributed on machines of the same type (for example, IBM 9370xx) and that the database software is the same everywhere (for example, SQL/DS). Furthermore, suitable communications software must be available, allowing one machine to activate another, make it perform a job, and transfer the result back again. CICS/ISC from IBM is such a tool. We refer to this solution as a "homogeneous" distributed database. The alternative is a "heterogeneous" distributed database involving hardware and software of different kinds and types.

We also assume that the speed and type of communications do not matter. Obviously, this is not true in on-line transaction-based systems. Not only would response times increase with slow communications, but also global deadlock would probably soon occur, blocking all processes because some outside transaction is too slow delivering its information.

We can illustrate the idea of distributed systems by extending our example. Suppose the sports equipment company decides to expand and establish local centers, thus transforming a small, profitable operation into a behemoth money-loser. It forms independent sales and administrative units in San Francisco, Los Angeles, and Sacramento with San Francisco as headquarters. The inventory is located in Sacramento because of low warehousing costs.

One advantage of the distributed solution is that data can be stored and processed where it belongs physically and logically. Thus each unit keeps track of its own employees, customers, orders, and so on. Logical and physical database designs can be adapted to local needs. The local units are in principle autonomous, meaning that they can function on their own without the others. The limitation on the functioning is that the inventory is not distributed. However, just as branch banks can handle minor transactions even though the central computer is unavailable, the individual units can function independently at a low activity level. In other words, they can enter orders into a local file and then have it uploaded to the central inventory records after recovery. Presumably, the company limits the size of the orders local units can handle in this way.

The local units themselves maintain applications, perform log and archival routines, and do other tasks. So far, the solution is distributed only in name, as what we have are several centralized systems.

The major change compared to other configurations is that individual units can search in, create in, and delete from databases belonging to the other units. Thus data is a common resource. For example, consider the following situations:

- An end user in San Francisco can order sweatshirts without knowing that the inventory table is in Sacramento.

- An applications programmer can write programs without worrying about where data is actually stored.

- The headquarters in San Francisco can fetch data stored locally to print bills, pay salaries, report taxes, and generate purchase orders and checks.

We can specify the major requirement for the distributed database as follows. It must demonstrate location transparency, so that users see no difference between remote and local transactions. A search of local employee records works the same (except perhaps faster) as one of remote inventory records. Distribution is thus a problem for the system, not for the end users or programmers.

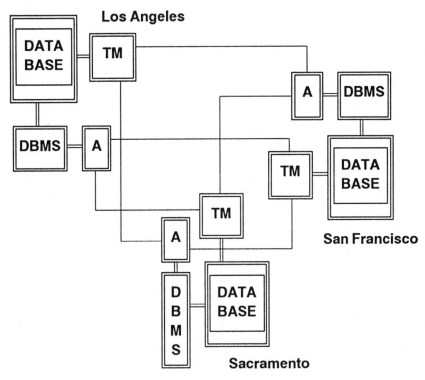

Figure 12-5. Example distributed configuration. TM: Transaction Manager, A: agent.

Figure 12-5 shows the distributed configuration. The two new system elements are a "transactions manager" (TM) at each local node and an "agent" (A) at each local DBMS. The function of a transactions manager depends on how the distributed system is implemented. The following example where a user in Los Angeles searches for golf balls (in stock in Sacramento) illustrates how work proceeds. A local customer (customer_no = 1001) has ordered golf balls and wants to know the balance (order_no = 2020). We use the following abbreviations: TM for Transactions Manager, A for Agent, and TM(San Francisco) for the specific TM located in San Francisco.

Suppose the user in San Francisco issues the following SQL command:

```
SELECT os.quantity * i.price
FROM inventory i, order_specs os
WHERE os.order_no = 2020
AND i.item_name = 'Golf balls'
```

We use standard SQL to process queries in relational distributed systems. The one extension we need is to include the node as part of the identification of individual tables.

The operation proceeds as follows:

1. TM(San Francisco) analyzes the command, then directs the transaction (or partial transactions) to the agents of the other nodes. TM(San Francisco) must know where the inventory and orderspec tables are. We describe how it knows this later. For now, assume it knows that the inventory table is in Sacramento and order_specs is local. TM(San Francisco) refers the job of finding the price of golf balls to the Agent in Sacramento.

2. A(Sacramento) acts on behalf of the TM who activated it. It confers with the local DBMS and makes it act as though the transaction were local:

```
SELECT price FROM inventory WHERE item_name =
'Golf balls'
```

3. When DBMS(Sacramento) finishes handling the transaction, the result (the price) must be sent on to TM(Sacramento) which analyzes it and relays it to A(San Francisco). A(San Francisco) then analyzes the reply, saves the result in a buffer, and lets the job proceed to the DBMS(San Francisco).

4. DBMS(San Francisco) must now issue:

```
SELECT quantity * SanF(result)
FROM order_specs
WHERE order_no = 2020
```

SanF(result) is the reply from the inventory.

The above transaction involves two nodes. Transactions may, however, involve partial results from several nodes that may have to be joined. Thus several agents, TMs, and DBMSes may all be active. The added complexity here is the locks that must be set and the logs that must be updated.

Global System Catalog

A key question raised in the last section was how TM(San Francisco) knew where the required tables were. Several solutions exist, all involving the distribution of the global system catalog.

One solution is for each TM to have its own system catalog plus copies of the ones belonging to other TMs. Together they form the global system catalog. The precise term is that we have **replicated** the catalog. So TM(San Francisco) can determine from the global system catalog that it must send the inquiry on to Sacramento. A variation is for the local DBMS to first send the transaction on for further processing by its own TM when it recognizes that it cannot handle the job.

The problem with copying system catalogs is that a superior authority must track all changes in their logical designs. The authority must, furthermore, ensure that all changes are copied to the other local databases.

Another solution is for individual TMs to only keep track of their own system catalogs. They then must examine the catalogs of the other TMs before starting a search. If, for example, data is distributed on five machines, a TM may have to search up to five other system catalogs to find what it wants.

A third solution is for one TM to have the global system catalog. All others then know where to search for information. One drawback to this solution is that, if the TM with the global system catalog fails, no one will be able to search the distributed data. So there must be at least one copy of the global catalog elsewhere for backup and fault tolerance.

Note that distributed systems are more complex in many ways than centralized ones. During the design stage, developers must decide on policies for distributing data and managing the system catalog. The programming of transaction managers and agents is a difficult job at best. The problems are even greater if the distributed system is "heterogeneous", meaning that it involves different hardware and software at different nodes.

On the other hand, the distributed system has many advantages. From the organization's point of view, it is efficient and secure to have data stored where it is most needed and where the capacity to handle it (for example, via statistical analysis) is the greatest. Distributed systems make it possible to store data in one place but manipulate it elsewhere. The local unit can handle its own functions independently, and can decide on its own computing policies as long as they do not affect other nodes.

From a security viewpoint, an advantage is that all archives and logs can be on other machines. So if one fails, the system can perform transactions securely from another machine while the first one is being repaired or reactivated. System crashes do not produce an insecure state that outside agents can attack easily.

As mentioned previously, distribution of data means distribution of responsibility. Furthermore, it also means that the local units must have knowledgeable people who can manage local computing. Note that this does not preclude centralization of applications development and maintenance.

In practice, the choice of configuration is not an either - or situation. One can design overall systems with both centralized and distributed features. For example, we could connect smaller units to a (for them) centralized database that actually is a node in a large distributed system.

Appendix A

Sample Database Tables

Table: employees

EMPLOYEE NO	FIRST NAME	LAST NAME	STREET	ZIP
12	Norman	Peterson	87 Main Street	12701
14	Peter	Swan	17 Chestnut Ave.	12010
15	Ursula	Klein	82 Violet Ave.	14031
17	Ivan	Jacobs	67 Elinore Ave.	14340
18	Joan	Smith	81 Bellis Street	14150
19	Allan	Larimer	2 Turkey Lane	14250
22	Henry	Jones	65 Birch Street	14760
26	Stephanie	Nickels	2 Blueberry Street	14031
27	George	Madison	3 Axle Street	14150
31	Harry	Blomberg	12 Factory Street	14802
33	Paul	Gilbert	4 Iris Avenue	14250
56	Michael	Olson	12 Hillside Street	14250

The remainder of the fields in the employee table:

E = employee number

DEPT = department

TYPE: D=Dealer, M=Manager, S=Salesperson

E	TELEPHONE	DATE_HIRED	TYPE	DEPT	BASE_PAY
12	316-4372	01-JAN-86	M	A40	1800
14	315-6566	22-APR-88	S	A40	1650
15	324-5262	01-JAN-86	M	A30	1800
17	339-7654	25-JUN-86	D		1200
18	337-2154	15-JUN-87	S	A20	1650
19	331-9191	01-FEB-88	S	A20	1650
22	332-2324	25-JUN-88	D		1200
26	325-5464	26-AUG-88	S	A30	1650
27	332-3344	01-APR-88	S	A20	1650
31	331-2030	10-SEP-87	D		1200
33	339-4354	15-AUG-85	M	A20	1800
56	332-3243	12-JUN-85	S	A20	1650

Table: inventory

ITEM NO	ITEM_NAME	QUANTITY ON HAND	PRICE	ORDER LEVEL
4012	Caddies	2	120.00	1
4013	Golf balls	545	2.00	250

ITEM NO	ITEM_NAME	QUANTITY ON HAND	PRICE	ORDER LEVEL
4014	Flags (golf)	180	5.00	48
4017	Green clipper	20	4.40	15
4018	Putter	30	89.00	25
4019	Tee	743	1.20	250
4022	Net (basketball)	20	35.70	5
4024	Shoes (basketball)	100	43.00	20
4028	Jersey (basketball)	22	18.90	20
4029	Basketballs	22	30.00	20
4031	Handball nets	21	78.60	12
4033	Handballs (men)	56	23.10	20
4034	Handballs (women)	34	32.10	20
4036	Handball goals	4	234.20	2
4052	Skipping rope (8 ft.)	124	1.70	25
4053	Skipping rope (10 ft.)	194	2.20	25
4056	Soccer ball	103	43.70	25
4057	Soccer net	10	97.50	4
4066	Volleyball	12	20.00	10
4077	Tennis balls (white)	253	10.40	20
4078	Tennis balls (yellow)	204	10.40	45
4079	Sweatbands	30	1.20	10
4082	Socks	298	4.50	30
4083	Shorts (small)	39	8.20	20

ITEM NO	ITEM_NAME	QUANTITY ON HAND	PRICE	ORDER LEVEL
4085	Shorts (medium)	34	10.00	30
4086	Blouses (small)	124	16.40	30
4087	Blouses (medium)	204	17.80	20
4088	Blouses (large)	54	19.80	25
4091	Tennis racket	25	43.00	20
4092	Badminton racket	34	29.80	20
4093	Tennis racket	20	67.40	18
4094	Tennis net	17	43.60	18

Table: Zip Codes (all in the state of New York)

ZIP CODE	CITY
12010	Amsterdam
12240	Albany
12610	Poughkeepsie
12701	Monticello
14031	Clarence
14150	Tonawanda
14250	Buffalo
14340	Niagara Falls
14760	Olean
14802	Alfred

Table: orders

ORDER NO	CUSTOMER NO	EMPLOYEE NO	RECEIVED	SHIPPED
2001	1002	33	03-AUG-89	15-AUG-89
2002	1005	33	04-AUG-89	17-AUG-89
2003	1003	22	08-AUG-89	30-AUG-89
2004	1001	15	08-AUG-89	30-AUG-89
2005	1003	22	10-AUG-89	16-AUG-89
2006	1004	12	11-AUG-89	13-AUG-89
2007	1006	33	12-AUG-89	16-AUG-89
2008	1002	56	16-AUG-89	24-AUG-89
2009	1003	22	17-AUG-89	01-SEP-89
2010	1003	22	19-AUG-89	22-AUG-89
2011	1004	12	21-AUG-89	30-AUG-89
2012	1001	15	22-AUG-89	28-AUG-89
2015	1001	15	23-AUG-89	29-AUG-89
2016	1002	56	25-AUG-89	30-AUG-89
2018	1002	56	27-AUG-89	03-SEP-89

Table: order_specs (order specifications)

ORDER_NO	ITEM_NO	QUANTITY
2001	4056	5
2001	4086	24
2001	4087	24
2001	4088	24
2002	4022	4
2002	4024	12
2002	4028	12
2002	4029	7
2003	4056	2
2004	4033	10
2004	4056	20
2005	4052	30
2005	4053	30
2006	4033	20
2006	4034	20
2006	4036	2
2007	4013	200
2007	4014	18
2007	4018	2
2007	4019	25

ORDER_NO	ITEM_NO	QUANTITY
2008	4033	7
2008	4034	20
2008	4056	10
2009	4034	3
2009	4053	12
2009	4056	3
2009	4066	3
2010	4056	4
2010	4077	17
2011	4029	7
2011	4053	4
2011	4083	31
2011	4085	10
2011	4086	12
2012	4034	7
2012	4077	10
2012	4078	16
2012	4079	200
2012	4093	2
2015	4034	10
2015	4053	30
2016	4031	4
2016	4057	2

ORDER_NO	ITEM_NO	QUANTITY
2016	4085	12
2018	4024	20
2018	4053	12
2018	4056	3
2018	4066	12
2018	4083	30

Table: customers

CNO = CUSTOMER_NO
T = TYPE: C = Club, E=Exercise Studio, R = Retailer, S = School
ZIP = ZIP_CODE

CNO	COMPANY NAME	STREET	ZIP	PHONE	T
1001	South Ball Club	1 Club St.	14031	327-5432	C
1002	East Side Club	65 High St.	14250	339-8070	C
1003	Lehigh High School	76 Farm St.	14031	323-4354	S
1004	Jack's Exercise Studio	56 Rye Lane	12610	349-2146	E
1005	Downtown Sport Shop	12 Bay Ave.	14150	357-2121	R
1006	Runners Unlimited	76 Gray St.	14340	331-1111	R

Appendix B

Syntax Conventions

The book uses the following notation:

Uppercase   Reserved words, such as CREATE TABLE. When issuing commands, however, case has no significance.

...   Indicates that the preceding text can be repeated.

[ ]   Indicates that the enclosed text is optional.

{ }   Indicates a group or sequence of elements. For example, {,field_name} indicates a sequence consisting of a comma followed by a field name.

| Indicates a choice (either-or). Either the item to the left of the line or the one to the right can be selected.

A typical example is:

```
SELECT  [ * | field_name [,field_name]...]
FROM table_name [,table_name]...
[ WHERE conditions ]
[ GROUP BY field_name [,field_name]...
[ HAVING conditions ]]
```

A command consists of a reserved word indicating its type. In addition, it may have a sequence of clauses, some of which **must** appear, whereas others (in brackets) are optional.

A clause (or supplementary specification to a command) consists of a type, plus predicates that specify the conditions under which it is executed. A condition is a statement that can only be true, false, or unknown. It will, therefore, always contain at least one arithmetic, logical, or relational operator (+, *, >, <, =, AND, OR, etc.).

The command here is SELECT. It must be followed by field names that specify the elements (table variables or constants) to be printed. An asterisk (*) or a field name must appear after it. The ellipsis in the item to the right of the vertical line indicates that several field names may appear.

Next the reserved word FROM must appear. It must be followed by table names. The WHERE clause is optional. If it appears, it must be followed by a condition.

If a GROUP BY clause appears, it must be followed by field names that indicate how to group the printout.

HAVING may appear, but since it is outside the brackets associated with GROUP BY, it can appear only if GROUP BY also appears.

Glossary

Access   Gain entry into something, such as a memory or disk location. The access time is how long it takes to find a piece of data in storage.

After image file   Part of the log containing data that has just been altered.

ANSI/SPARC   American National Standards Institute / System Planning and Requirements Committee.

ASC   Abbreviation for ascending.

ASCII   American Standard Code for Information Interchange.

Atomic   Indivisible. A field value that cannot be reduced to a set of data values of the same type. The opposite is non-atomic.

Attribute   Value that describes something, can be translated by a field in a table. It is characterized by the fact that its range is an atomic domain.

Before image file (or **shadow pages**)   Part of the log that contains the data as it appeared before it was altered.

Bits per second (bps)   A specification of the data transfer rate on a communication line. High rates are specified in Mbps (M = Mega = 1 million).

Block The basic unit of data transfer between the physical storage medium and computer memory. Typical sizes are 1K, 2K, or 4K.

Buffer Memory used to save data blocks, such as ones consisting of data that has just been referenced. Buffers are also used when data is read from mass storage (such as a hard disk) faster than the CPU can handle it.

Byte Basic unit of storage in a computer, consists of 8 bits.

Cartesian product Set composed of the product of two sets. The result is a new set of all possible element pairs.

Cluster A physical storage technique whereby logically associated records are stored together in mass storage. The process is "clustering". If only one table is involved, it is "intrafile clustering", whereas, if several are involved, it is "interfile clustering".

CODASYL COonference on DAta SYstem Languages. Often used specifically to refer to the Data Base Task Group (DBTG).

CPU Central Processing Unit. The control unit of the computer that fetches, decodes, and executes instructions.

Cursor A pointer that indicates where an activity will occur. In a database, a pointer to the location in the physically stored table (file) where the next operation will occur.

DA See DBA.

Dataspace An address space in which the correspondence between the logical tables and their placement in physical blocks is maintained.

DBA or DA Database Administrator. The person responsible for operating and maintaining a database.

DBMS Data Base Management System. Program that defines databases and stores and retrieves data.

DCL Data Control Language. The part of the data sub-language that deals with access rights to the database.

DDL Data Definition Language. The part of the data sub-language that deals with the creation and alteration of the table structure.

DESC Abbreviation for descending.

Disk A physical mass storage device.

Disk driver The program in the operating system that reads data from and writes data to the physical mass storage devices.

DML Data Manipulation Language. The part of the data sub-language that deals with manipulation of the data in the tables.

Domain The set of permissible values for an attribute.

DRDBMS Distributed Relational DataBase Management System.

Equijoin A natural join where equality between two join predicates is sought.

File manager The program or procedure that handles the task of associating logical tables with a dataspace.

Foreign key A field in an owned table that presupposes the existence of a value in another table (an owner table).

Fragmentation An indication of the degree to which logically associated data is spread out on the disk.

Indexing   Search strategy whereby individual records are found indirectly by searching through an index table generated for the purpose.

Integrity   The requirement that a database must contain data in accordance with its intended application.

Interfile clustering   See clustering.

Intrafile clustering   See clustering.

I/O operations   Input/output operations. The process by which the computer reads from and writes to the peripherals such as a disk.

Join predicate   Fields that make it possible to combine records from various tables.

KB   Kilobyte. 1024 bytes.

LAN   Local Area Network. A network in which the distance between individual units (nodes) is less than a few hundred meters.

Lock   A mark applied to a set of records to prevent certain actions from being performed on it.

Log   A file that records all changes performed on the data in a database.

Logical   Defined, as opposed to the existing or physical. A logical database is thus the definition, not the physically existing database. The logical database consists of table definitions, whereas the physical one is data stored bit by bit in mass storage.

Mainframe   Large computer capable of performing substantial data processing tasks.

MB   Megabyte. 1024 KB = 1,048,576 bytes.

Natural join   The combination of tables via a join predicate. It removes one join predicate in the result table.

NULL   A data value that is neither true nor false. A nonexistent value or empty field.

OS/2   Operating System 2. Microsoft operating system for IBM's PS/2 computers and compatibles.

Page   Synonym for block.

PCTFREE   The parameter that indicates how much memory is available in the individual physical blocks to be kept free for later data updates.

Physical   **See** logical.

Pointer   A variable containing the address of a value.

Primary key   A field or combination of fields that identifies each individual record uniquely.

Query   A search, but used generally to indicate any manipulation of the objects in a database.

RAM   Ordinary (read/write) memory, the working memory of the computer or the primary storage area.

RDBMS   Relational DBMS.

Redundancy   The same information stored in several places.

RID   Record IDentification. A value that indicates the address of a record. It designates the block in which the record lies and its precise location within the block.

SAA   Systems Application Architecture. A definition of a common interface between various IBM products and platforms.

Sequential   A sequence of actions, such as I/O reads of one physical block after the other.

SQL   Structured Query Language.

SQL/DS   Structured Query Language/Data System, IBM's SQL dialect and DBMS.

SQL*Forms   Oracle's application for creating screen images for user interfaces.

SQL*Plus   SQL dialect marketed by Oracle Corporation.

Synchronization point (syncpoint)   The moment when the DBMS updates the database. It involves the writing of the log and the buffer contents onto disk.

Trigger   An event that causes an action or series of actions to be performed.

Validity check   A routine that examines a data value to determine whether it is correct. For example, it might check whether a month is a whole number between 1 and 12 inclusive.

VM   Virtual Machine, an IBM mainframe operating system.

Note: For more complete and extensive definitions of database terms, see E. Thro, *The Database Dictionary* (San Marcos, CA: Microtrend Books, 1990).

Bibliography

ANSI Inc.,
American National Standard for Information Systems, Database Language-SQL, ANSI X3.135-1986. New York, 1986.

Bisland, R.B., Jr
Developing Application Systems Using Oracle, Prentice-Hall, Englewood Cliffs, NJ, 1989.

Ceri, S. and G. Pelagatti
Distributed Databases. McGraw-Hill, New York, 1984.

Codd, E. F.
"A Relational Model of Data for Large Shared Data Banks," *CACM* 13:6, June 1970.

Codd, E. F.
The Relational Model for Database Management, Version 2, Addison-Wesley, Reading, MA, 1990.

Date, C. J.
An Introduction to Database Systems, 5th ed. Addison-Wesley, Reading, MA, 1990, Vols. 1 and 2.

Date, C. J.
A Guide to the SQL Standard, 2nd ed. Addison-Wesley, Reading, MA, 1989.

Date, C. J. and C. White.
A Guide to SQL/DS. Addison-Wesley, Reading, MA, 1988.

Dutka, A. F. and H. H. Hanson.
Fundamentals of Data Normalization. Addison-Wesley, Reading, MA, 1989.

Edwards, J. B. "High Performance Without Compromise,"
Datamation, July 1, 1990, pp. 53-58.

Elmasri, R. A. and S. B. Navathe.
Fundamentals of Database Systems. Benjamin/Cummings, Redwood City, CA, 1989.

Emerson, S. et al.
The Practical SQL Handbook. Addison-Wesley, Reading, MA, 1989.

Everest, G. C.
Database Management. McGraw-Hill, New York, 1986.

Fleming, C. and B. Von Halle.
Handbook of Relational Database Design. Addison-Wesley, Reading, MA, 1989.

Fosdick, H.
OS/2 Database Manager: A Developer's Guide, Wiley, New York, 1989.

Kent, W.
"A Simple Guide to Five Normal Forms in Relational Database Theory," *CACM* 26:2, February 1983.

Kung, C.
"Object Subclass Hierarchy in SQL: A Simple Approach," *CACM* 33:7, July 1990, pp. 117-125.

Lorie, R. and J. J. Daudenarde.
SQL and its Applications. Prentice-Hall, Englewood Cliffs, NJ, 1990.

Marlyn, T. and T. Hartley.
DB2 SQL: A Professional Programmer's Guide.
Intertext/McGraw-Hill, New York, 1989.

Perry, J. T. and J. G. Lateer
Understanding Oracle. Sybex, San Francisco, CA, 1989.

VanDerLans, R.
Introduction to SQL. Addison-Wesley, Reading, MA, 1988.

Wiederhold, G.
File Organization for Database Design, McGraw-Hill, New York, 1987.

Trademark List

AT	IBM
Database Services	Microsoft
dBASE	Ashton-Tate
DB2	IBM
IMS	IBM
MS-DOS	Microsoft
MVS	IBM
Oracle	Oracle
OS/2	Microsoft
OS/2 Database Manager	Microsoft
OS/2 Extended Edition	Microsoft
PC	IBM
PRO*xxx	Oracle
PS/2	IBM
QM	Microsoft
QMF	IBM
Query Management Facility	IBM

Query Manager(QM)	Microsoft
REXX	IBM
SAA	IBM
SQL*Calc	Oracle
SQL*CASE	Oracle
SQL/DS	IBM
SQL*Forms	Oracle
SQL*Menu	Oracle
SQL*Plus	Oracle
SQL*Report	Oracle
System R	IBM
Systems Application Architecture	IBM
UNIX	AT&T
VM	IBM
VM/CMS	IBM
VM/SP	IBM

Index

* (all fields), 29, 31
* (in COUNT), 51
: (screen field names), 232
: (SQL variables), 191, 206
. (table name separator), 47
% (any string), 33, 37
_ (any character), 33

A

Abbreviations for table names, 25-
    26, 47 (*see also* synonyms)
Access control (to objects), 87-94
    auditing, 113-115
    example, 89-92
    extending rights, 90-94
    matrix, 88-89
    purpose, 87-88
Access matrix, 88-89
Access module, 186-187
Access strategy, 97
ACQUIRE DBSPACE, 249, 261
ADD DBSPACE, 249
Adding fields, 23
ADD PRIMARY KEY, 159

After image file, 175, 176
Agents, 283-285
Algebraic operators, 59
ALL, 55
All fields (*), 29, 31
Allocations schema, 279
All records, deleting, 66
ALTER TABLE, 23-24, 159
Ambiguous names, 47
Analyzing SQL commands,
    186-187
AND, 29-30
ANSI/SPARC, 6, 245-246
ANSI SQL standard, 9
ANY, 55
Any character (_), 33
Any string (%), 33, 37
Applications, 221-240
    OS/2 Database Manager,
        222-228
    SQL*Forms, 228-240
Applications of databases, 10,
    267-268
Applications programmers, 3
Architectural model, 241-242

The *Data Based Advisor®* Series
Lance A. Leventhal, Ph.D., Series Director

Designing User Interfaces

by James E. Powell

User interfaces are often the key to the success or failure of software. Today's users demand software that is easy to learn, intuitive, and efficient. Experienced program designer James E. Powell provides a thorough, common-sense approach to creating effective user interfaces. Drawing from real-world applications, he asks readers to apply design techniques and compare their results with recommended solutions. The book covers user interface fundamentals, analyzing user needs, visual design, data entry, error handling, menus, help, graphics, output, installation, tutorials, user manuals and documentation, creativity, legal issues, and future directions.

Special features of the book are:

❑ Example programs using the popular FoxPro database manager.

❑ Many practical examples and sample problems drawn from actual applications.

❑ Extensive discussions of seldom described topics, such as error handling, data entry design, help design, installation design, tutorial design, and considerations for handicapped users.

❑ Emphasis on a friendly interface with gentle tone and non-antagonistic approach.

❑ Descriptions of methods for creating interfaces for both beginners and experienced users.

❑ Thorough coverage of visual design, windowing, menus, graphical interfaces, and output design.

About the Author:

James E. Powell is a program designer with over 15 years of practical experience. He is also a contributing Editor to Puget Sound Computer User.

7 x 9, 448 pages, trade paperback, ISBN: 0-915391-40-6, $27.95, **Order # MT40**

Available from your favorite book or computer store, use the order form at the end of this book, or telephone 1 (800) SLAWSON.

Slawson Communications • 165 Vallecitos de Oro • San Marcos, CA 92069-1436

From the Lance A. Leventhal Microtrend™ Series,
A complete, one-stop reference guide to all aspects of IBM PC and PS/2 graphics.

IBM PC and PS/2 Graphics Handbook

Ed Teja and Laura Johnson

This single source will answer all your questions about what the standards are, what works with what, what features languages and operating systems offer, how to upgrade systems, what to buy for specific applications and requirements, and how to make programs run on a variety of computers. The book contains many easily referenced tables and charts for quick access and rapid comparisons of systems, hardware, programs, and standards.

Special features of the book are:

- ❏ Covers adapters, monitors, printers, standards, file formats, languages, and applications packages.

- ❏ Includes summaries, a resource list, a glossary, an acronym list, and an annotated bibliography.

- ❏ Focuses on widely used hardware and software for word processing, business graphics, presentation graphics, CAD/CAM/CAE, and desktop publishing.

- ❏ Emphasizes current and emerging standards, such as VGA, 8514/A, Multisync monitors, GKS, IGES, TIFF, Borland Graphics Interface, Microsoft Windows, and Presentation Manager.

- ❏ Describes how to identifify the graphics adapter on a system and how to convert between different screen and printer aspect ratios.

Ed Teja and Laura Johnson have been writing professionally about computers and electronics since 1976. A former computer and peripherals editor for *EDN* magazine, Teja has written articles for more than 35 magazines and has published three books.

7 x 9, 480 pages, trade paperback, index. ISBN 0-915391-35-X $24.95
Order # MT35

Available from your favorite book or computer store, use the order form at the end of the book, or telephone 1 (800) SLAWSON.

Slawson Communications • 165 Vallecitos de Oro • San Marcos, CA 92069-1436

The *Data Based Advisor*® Series
Lance A. Leventhal, Ph.D., Series Director

Clipper Programming Guide, 2nd Edition

by Rick Spence

Nantucket's Clipper compiler for dBASE programs has become one of the most popular productivity tools in the database world. This Second Edition of Rick Spence's best-seller covers the new Version 5 of Clipper. It includes extensive new material on linking, scoping, preprocessors, multi-dimensional arrays, color management, screen capture, word processing, data dictionaries, primary and foreign keys, referential integrity, and multiple linked relationships. It also has expanded coverage of error handling, help systems, pulldown menus, message and dialog systems, and C data structures. Even more on Clipper internals, direct file access, networking, and C programming. Contains many examples drawn from actual applications and extensive discussions of all aspects of programming.

Special features of the book are:

❑ Timely coverage, deals with all features of Version 5.

❑ Explains how to use Clipper on local area networks.

❑ Detailed examples showing the use of C with Clipper.

❑ Description of advanced query techniques involving multiple databases and multiple relations.

❑ Extensive set of utilities for viewing all types of Clipper files.

About the Author:

Rick Spence is currently an independent consultant specializing in database applications and Unix systems. He was a member of the Nantucket development team and a co-developer of Clipper. He is the author of the monthly "Hardcore Clipper" column in Data Based Advisor and an expert columnist in Reference (Clipper) magazine.

7 x 9, 700 pages, trade paperback, ISBN: 0-915391-41-4, $27.95
Publication Date: 12/1/90, **Order # MT41**
Available from your favorite book or computer store, use the order form at the end of this book, or telephone 1 (800) SLAWSON.

Slawson Communications • 165 Vallecitos de Oro • San Marcos, CA 92069-1436

The *Data Based Advisor*® Series
Lance A. Leventhal, Ph.D., Series Director

Clipper Developer's Library

by James Occhiogrosso
Consultant James Occhiogrosso provides an extensive add-on library for Clipper 5.0, comparable to libraries costing hundreds of dollars. Contains working functions that perform application management, array manipulation, database operations, data conversion, data entry and validation, date and time manipulation, development support, environment control, file operations, keyboard control, memo handling, network operations, printer control, and screen manipulation. All programs are also available on disk.

Special features of the book are:

❑ All routines are selected from working Clipper applications.

❑ Provides complete source code and a royalty-free distribution license.

❑ Contains detailed instructions for using each function and examples of typical applications.

❑ Explains how to create, use, and maintain program libraries.

About the Author:

James Occhiogrosso is an independent consultant specializing in order tracking and accounting systems for small business. An experienced Clipper consultant, he has worked with the program for many years on a variety of applications. He has also been active in Clipper user groups.

7 x 9, 700 pages, trade paperback ISBN 0-915391-39-2, $29.95
Publication Date: 2/1/91, **Order # MT39**

Available from your favorite book or computer store,
use order form at end of book, or telephone 1 (800) SLAWSON.

**Slawson Communications • 165 Vallecitos de Oro • San Marcos, CA
92069-1436**

Order Form

Thank you for purchasing this Microtrend™ book. To order additional copies of this book or any of our other titles, please complete the form below, or call **1-800-SLAWSON**.

Name _____

Address _____

City/State/Zip _____

Qty	Order #	Title	Price Each	Total
		Subtotal		
		Sales Tax: CA residents add 7.25%		
		Shipping Charge: $3.50 per book		
		TOTAL		

U.S. Shipping

Books are shipped UPS except when a post office box is given as delivery address.

Form of Payment

☐ Visa ☐ MasterCard ☐ Check

Card #: ☐☐☐☐ ☐☐☐☐ ☐☐☐☐ ☐☐☐☐

Expiration date: _____

Signature: _____ Date _____

Mail your order to:

Microtrend™ Books
Slawson Communications, Inc.
Dept DUI
165 Vallecitos de Oro
San Marcos, CA 92069-1436
619/744-2299

Reader Comments
SQL and Relational Databases

This book has been edited, the edited material reviewed, and the program matter tested and checked for accuracy, but bugs find their way into books as well as software. Please take a few minutes to tell us if you have found any errors, and give us your general comments regarding the quality of this book. Your time and attention will help us improve this and future products.

Did you find any mistakes? _____YES_____

Is this book complete? (If not, what should be added?) ___No___

What do you like about this book? ___NOT A LOT___

What do you not like about this book? ___EVERYTHING___

What other books would you like to see developed? ___ANYTHING BUT SQL OR DBMS___

Other comments: ___THIS BOOK SHOULD BE BURNED___

If you would like to be notified about new editions of this and/or other books that may be of interest to you, please complete the following:

Name _____ME_____
Address _____HERE_____
City/State/Zip _____?_____

Mail to:

Microtrend™ Books
Slawson Communications, Inc.
165 Vallecitos de Oro
San Marcos, CA 92069-1436